109

WHAT IS PHILOSOPHY?

What is Philosophy?

A MARXIST INTRODUCTION

by Howard Selsam

AUTHOR OF
"SOCIALISM AND ETHICS"

International Publishers   New York

To Millicent

CONTENTS

INTRODUCTION   9

I. *PHILOSOPHY FOR WHOM?*   17

II. *MATERIALISM AND IDEALISM*   39

III. *PERMANENCE AND CHANGE*   77

IV. *THE MEANING OF SCIENCE*   112

V. *HISTORY AND FREEDOM*   148

REFERENCES   187

INTRODUCTION

THE PURPOSE of this book is to give to that increasing body of men and women interested in theoretical questions, some idea as to what philosophy is and some indication of how it can be used in dealing with the practical and theoretical questions that confront us. It is not the purpose of the author to bring philosophy down to earth, but to show that it has always been there. However abstract philosophical speculations may seem, the different systems and types of philosophy have been just so many ways in which men have reacted to the world of nature and society around them. Today, as perhaps never before, conflicting social attitudes and movements tend to generate conflicting philosophies, theories, or as they are often called, ideologies. And conversely, different conceptions of the world and of man tend to guide their followers into different paths of action. Aristocrats and bourgeois democrats, reactionaries and progressives, capitalists and class-conscious workers, believe in, and act upon, different theories of nature and of human life. Undoubtedly, the professor dismissed from Yale University for his progressive teachings and actions has a different world-view from that of the gentlemen who desired his removal. The trade union pickets at the gates of mines and factories differ in their conception of right and wrong, human nature and human good, from the deputy sheriffs and vigilantes who assault them. Philosophy (which, it must be remembered, is only a general term for these various world-views taken in their historical development) has acquired a new importance for our generation; not because of the activity of our so-called philosophers, but rather because our time demands that the great masses of people find their way about amidst the present strife of forces and theories.

Someone once said that a landlady interviewing a prospective lodger asks him many unimportant questions but neglects the essential one: "What is your philosophy?" If that is true, how much more important is it for us to know something of the philosophy of the man whom we elect President of the United States, or head of a trade union. When we learn not to shy away from the name of philosophy, we will discover that it is merely the study of the most basic characteristics of both the world and man, and is intimately bound up with the social movements of all times.

It is a sad and doubtful tribute to most past philosophy that the expression "taking a thing philosophically" has come to mean taking it as it is, without protest; accepting whatever befalls as inevitable and unavoidable. To take hunger or unemployment or fascism "philosophically" has become equivalent to resigned acceptance. Yet philosophy has a more significant meaning than that implied by the above expression. To be philosophical in this other sense does not imply abject resignation, but rather the power to analyze clearly our aims, their practicability, and the means necessary to realize them. In either case we all have a philosophy, and that philosophy is the theory of our action. The first attitude has become identified with philosophy itself, perhaps, because so much philosophy has tended to provide a justification of the social order as it happened to exist at any given time.

This volume seeks to provide its readers with some elementary aspects of a theory which not only can aid them in understanding themselves and their environment, but more important still, will help them to deal more effectively with it. It is the author's belief that philosophy is significant in the present world situation and will count for still more in the fight against war and fascism that confronts us. Nearly a century ago Karl Marx recognized the importance of philosophy in the struggles first of the German commercial and industrial classes against the feudal aristocracy which hindered their development, and later in the struggles of the working class of all countries for liberation from the forces that oppressed them. Thus, for the first time in history, a philosophy was developed for those nameless masses who, hitherto, had no body of theory which they could truly call their own. It is the primary purpose of this book to introduce the reader to this new and important philosophy—dialectical materialism—in the hope that its further study will illumine and clarify both his relations to, and responsibilities in, changing contemporary society.

The first chapter will seek to throw light on the nature and the problems of philosophy as a social-historical enterprise. This is a necessary step, for without some knowledge of how philosophy arose and developed, and how it was influenced by and in turn reacted upon changing social life, most of the value it can have for us today is lost. Some philosophers, it is true, disdain this, maintaining that the "truths" of philosophy, like those of revealed religion, are eternal and independent of human social processes. We shall seek to show that this idea, too, has its history, its social origins, and its implications for the pressing problems of our day. Finally, two more or less closely related questions must be examined: What have been the dominant conceptions on the part of philosophers of the purpose of philosophy, and how do these expressed purposes correspond with the actual function of various philosophies in human history? This analysis will lead us to the Marxist belief that since all historical society has been a scene of class struggle, philosophy, whatever else it has been, has served as the theoretical weapon of opposing classes and especially of the dominant class at any given time to maintain its privileged position. We shall see, finally, how Marx and Engels sought to provide an adequate philosophy for the working class in its struggles for better conditions and ultimately for socialism.

The second chapter deals with the major conflict in philosophy between materialism and idealism, and seeks to show the derivation of philosophical idealism from spiritualistic or religious views of the world. What does it mean in actual practice to take a materialist as against a spiritualist or idealist approach to the problems of life? The social consequences of these positions are analyzed, their virtues and limitations shown. This-worldliness and other-worldliness are presented and evaluated in terms of the ways they function in human society. Materialism is presented in contrast with ideal-ism both as a practical way of life and as a philosophical world-view. Throughout this chapter the attempt has been made to see the most general features of all idealist and of all materialist philosophies. This is not to imply that these two fundamentally opposed positions are each consistent and uniform or that there may not be con-siderable over-lapping. The following chapter, in fact, indicates divergencies within the materialist and idealist camps and exhibits dialectical materialism as the only philosophy which does justice both to the materiality, and to the temporal development of nature and society. The reason for this treatment is that we get a deeper understanding of the basic features of these two view-points by pulling them apart and exhibiting them in their sharpest oppositions.

In the third chapter two other opposed ways of view-ing the world are presented, namely, the static and the dynamic. Again, the social roots of these contrasted views are explored together with their implications for the world today. The problem is shown to take two related forms; first, a view of the world which ignores time and confines change to "appearance" only, versus the view which emphasizes time and the temporal move-ment of all things; second, abstract or mechanical modes of handling or interpreting things and events, which is

shown to be the heritage of the "timeless" view of the
universe, versus the dialectical conception of the nature
of all process and the dialectical method of dealing with
change. Aristotelian and Hegelian ways of interpreting
evolution are examined and applied to the problem of
the evolution of capitalism into socialism. The dialectical method is discussed briefly in both its Hegelian and
Marxist forms, and its application to social and other
problems is illustrated. The central point of the chapter
is that materialism is not enough, that the mechanical
materialism of the eighteenth century must give way to
dialectical materialism if social and scientific progress
is to be made.

Since dialectical materialism as a philosophy has been
shown to be inseparable from the sciences, and since
scientific knowledge is a necessary instrument for social
transformation, chapter four deals with some of the
aspects of science relevant to this whole discussion. How
did science arise in human history and what provided
the motive force for the acquisition of exact knowledge
of nature and man? What is the relation between theory
and practice in the growth of scientific knowledge? What
is the position of science in capitalist society today and
how does it fare under socialism? Science is distinguished from and related to ordinary beliefs held about
the phenomena of our world in an effort to indicate
what it is that makes any knowledge scientific. The
struggle of science and theological orthodoxy is examined, especially as revealed in the great philosophical
systems which attempted to reconcile them and in con-

temporary efforts to keep science from trespassing on the territory occupied by religious belief. The fight of reaction against science is exhibited on the new level it has reached since Marx's application of scientific method to political economy. Earlier, science challenged only the prevailing ideologies of existing societies, now Marxist science challenges the economic and political order itself. Finally, a brief account is given of dialectical materialism as a philosophy of science.

In the fifth and last chapter the various threads of the philosophical controversies discussed are brought together for an examination of the process of history and the nature of the good life. Contrasting theories of history, as well as completely non-historical theories of society, are analyzed. Hegel's philosophy of history is presented and criticized in terms of its inability to make its conceptions concrete and to solve the problem of the relation between the direction of history and the force which moves it in this direction. The Marxist conception of history, historical materialism, is developed as the science of historical movement. Here is found for the first time a completely materialist conception of history as a process having a direction which is determined by the very forces which move it forward. Is there really progress in history, in what does it consist, why is the working class the progressive force in the world today? These are a few of the questions examined in terms of historical materialism. But the answers to these questions imply a theory of ethics as the conception of the nature of the good life. Ethics and the philosophy of history are brought into unity through the idea of freedom as man's complete rational mastery of himself and his natural and social world for the fulfillment of his needs and desires. The socialist society is seen as the next step forward, as a step made inevitable by the contradictions of capitalism and attained through the struggles of the working class, in alliance with all progressive forces in society, for greater freedom.

In the ways described this book attempts to map out something of the field of philosophical discussion and to bring to a focus the major intellectual conflicts of our time. It does this materialistically through the examination of the social background of our philosophical ideas and for the purpose of providing us with a sound theory of the world which can serve as the basis of progressive social action.

I. PHILOSOPHY FOR WHOM?

THE CONTENT OF PHILOSOPHY — IS PHILOSOPHY DANGER-OUS? — SOCIAL ROOTS AND CONSEQUENCES — PHILOSOPHY AND THE SCIENCES — CHANGING PURPOSES OF PHILOSOPHY — THE GREEKS — LOCKE — FRENCH MATERIALISTS — HEGEL — MARX — DIALECTICAL MATERIALISM AS THE PHILOSOPHY OF THE WORKING CLASS

WHEN you wish to study physics, psychology, economics, or history you find a specific subject matter, a special body of knowledge available. But when you seek acquaintance with philosophy, you are confronted by a vast amount of literature that presents the widest diversity of matter and method.

Philosophy has been many different things to men in different ages. From its recorded birth in the Greek world of the sixth century before Christ to the present day it has taken such diverse forms and shapes that men sometimes say there is no one thing that can be called philosophy. It has seemed to be simply a long series of individual guesses of individual men as to what the world is, how and for what purpose men are, and what it is that makes a good life. The situation is indeed so scandalous that teachers of philosophy cannot agree among themselves as to the subject matter they teach, much less agree on the particular doctrines. It seems that there is nothing so absurd but that some philosopher has not held it to be the final and ultimate truth, or no institution or government so outworn or so oppressive but that some philosopher cannot find in it the final goal of creation. Seeing this sad condition, the pious return happily to their God, the cynical to their sneers, the scientist goes back to his laboratory, while the "level-headed" business man continues to seek profit —all alike shunning the windy speculations or crazy ideas of the "philosophers."

But philosophy cannot be escaped so easily. For these men, too, have a philosophy, regardless of the fact that they are not conscious of it. Philosophy is something that we all have, just as prose is something we all speak. Before there is conscious thought, before there is theory, there is practice. To sustain his life man is forced to cope with a complex, recalcitrant, and often hostile environment. Whether he lives by hunting or fishing, by clipping coupons or by tenant farming or factory labor, he performs acts, handles tools, enters into relationships which imply things concerning himself and the world he lives in. But as these rudimentary beliefs are the materials of philosophy, as the theory of the world and our life, philosophy is something no man can avoid and it would therefore appear better to inquire a little concerning it.

Men can be urged not to inquire into philosophy for two quite different reasons. First, because it is a little dangerous for people whose feet are not firmly rooted in the earth. They may lose themselves in abstract speculations and forget that philosophy is for life and not life for philosophy. I remember, for example, a young man just out of college who, having studied philosophy and having "learned" that nothing in the world exists but his own ideas, had determined to abolish the existing war, misery, and unemployment by committing suicide. Fortunately he reconsidered his premises and turned to more effective ways of eliminating these social ills. Secondly, and what is feared much more by those who caution against philosophy, is the fact that thinking seriously about such basic questions as philosophy concerns itself with may destroy religious or political orthodoxy. It is not philosophy as such that is here objected to but any philosophy other than the one that is supposed to be good for us to believe. It is for such reasons that until about 1880 almost no one was allowed to teach philosophy in an American college but the president, who was generally a professional theologian as well. Those groups or classes, then, which dominate any society must seek either to abolish the study of philosophy or else to control the study so that only the philosophy that is to their interest may be learned.

But is there any one thing called philosophy and is it something more than the mere thoughts of individual men? A survey of philosophies in their historical succession throws light on this question. The first Greek philosophers made what seem to us to be "guesses" concerning the nature of things and are described as having individual opinions. Thales said the stuff, the first principle, of all things is water. Anaximenes said it wasn't water but air, and later Heraclitus seems to have thought it was fire. These are not guesses, for of far greater importance than the superficial fact that these men thought differently is the fact that they asked a similar question, made similar presuppositions, and reached conclusions in accordance with the thought of their time. They assumed, for one thing, that all the diversity of living forms in the heavens and upon the earth are derived by an endless process of change from some common element. They assumed, secondly, that this common stuff from which all things had been derived was one of the four substances the Greeks regarded as basic—earth, air, fire, and water. Third, they assumed that this process of derivation of things from a common stuff happened *naturally,* that is, without any guidance or interference by the gods, and that it occurred according to some general principles or laws. Sketchy as this analysis is, it reveals something of importance, namely, that the differences among these thinkers were relatively unimportant in comparison with the things on which they agreed. When we turn to the later history of philosophy with all its complication of complicated systems, we find something strikingly similar. We find that behind all the apparent diversities there are some fundamental agreements, and that the assumptions which are made fall into a few fundamental clusters. More important than the answers philosophers have given are the questions they have asked, and many of the most difficult problems concerning the history of philosophy disappear when we approach the different systems in terms of the questions their respective authors asked concerning reality and truth.

Historical analysis reveals that diverse and opposed philosophies arise not by pure reason or by plain facts alone, but also because of conflicting social forces. Any study of the history of philosophy, any presentation of the philosophy of an individual or a period, which ignores the social setting of philosophies, the age, the economic system and economic conflicts, the group or class position of the philosopher, must inevitably fail to understand the cause of the divergencies and conflicts of philosophical systems. Such an approach fails, futher, to explain how and why it is that philosophy did not remain on the path that its earliest originators pursued, namely, an objective inquiry into nature such as is now represented by the sciences—why, in other words, philosophy developed as a study separate and independent, in large part, from science; sometimes close and sympathetic, sometimes openly hostile.

The history of philosophy in its context, the actual changing life of men in society, reveals that philosophy has been no merely "dispassionate" search for truth, but has frequently been interested in defending or attacking existing social institutions and traditions. The more minutely the quarrels and controversies of philosophers are analyzed the more clearly does it appear that behind them are different programs of social action, different approaches to pressing problems of the time. Unfortunately, this fact has been ignored in most histories of philosophy and it is for this very reason that so many of these great philosophical controversies sound empty and meaningless today. The most fundamental question in all the history of philosophy is the question as to whether that which is ultimately real (that is, that on which the existence of all things depends) is the material world around us of which we are a part, or is of the nature of mind, or a purely logical system of eternal and self-existent Ideas or principles. Examination reveals that this question is a direct reflection of social interests and conflicts. A second important question, that concerning the reality or unreality of movement, process, change, is likewise socially conditioned. Just how this is will be explained in the following chapters. The point to be kept in mind is that no philosophy is meaningless because all philosophies represent attitudes towards the world derived from particular social and historical influences. This latter point is true even though some few philosophies may have been developed primarily as justifications for their individual authors' type of life. For any individual's desired mode of life is itself socially conditioned and requires one organization of society rather than another for its fulfillment. All this is not to say that a man has first a clearly understood social position and then consciously develops a philosophy to justify it. The actual situation is generally far more complex. Ideas themselves, once they have arisen in human thought, become social influences and may help in determining the path an individual or group takes. The point is only that philosophies are inextricably bound up with the social environment, arising from it and reacting in turn upon it, and it is the knowledge of this relationship which clarifies their meaning.

The two problems that have been called the most fundamental in the history of philosophy—those of matter or mind and of permanence or change as constituting reality—raise the question of the relation of philosophy and science. Science deals with the things and events of our world as it finds them, and arises out of man's need and desire to predict and control his environment. Its business is to find out the nature of things, and the principles in accordance with which they operate. For science the problems are always concrete ones: is such-and-such the case, how do the observed changes actually come about, and how can such-and-such a desired state of things be brought about? But philosophy, developed ahead of science by the Greeks, was led to its different formulation of these questions by social influences. What was important for these philosophers was less the question of fact concerning what is real than it was the question of which things are to be valued or preferred above others. Plato, for example, in seeking to uphold the moral and political values of his class, and thus to preserve the *status quo,* sought to find them rooted in the eternal structure of the universe. This automatically took them away from the scrutiny and criticism of the ordinary citizen (not to mention the slave) and left them the province solely of the thinker, the gentleman of leisure who could spend his life in the contemplation of these eternal truths. Thus, at one and the same time, he made reality to consist in these changeless principles, only dimly manifested by our mundane material world, and set up the ideal of the aristocratic philosopher who, contemplating these truths, was alone capable of ruling society.

The relation between philosophy and the various sciences has been the source of endless disagreement, with philosophers almost always claiming the right to say the first and last words. It has already been suggested that philosophy is not always kindly disposed towards science, that in fact it has often been against science. Now science itself has social roots and is responsive to social influences. But science always means exact knowledge of selected aspects of our world (the aspects *selected* depending in the long run on the needs of commerce, industry, and technology in general) attained by means of careful observation and manipulation of the material concerning which knowledge is sought. Such knowledge is not always desired by those in positions of power because it may run counter to ideas and institutions they seek to perpetuate. The scientific knowledge of nature that was being gained, for example, in the sixteenth and seventeenth centuries by such men as Galileo and Descartes served the interests of the rising middle class which needed exact knowledge for navigation, warfare, mining enterprises, and so on. At the same time it was fought bitterly in the universities which were controlled by the feudal classes whose sole desire was to keep the existing economic order of society and therefore the dogmas of Christianity and the power of the church at Rome. In our own day we see that the science of race, included under anthropology, which tends increasingly to show the artificiality of racial boundaries and the essential equality of all races, is abhorred by the ruling capitalist clique of Germany which holds its power by turning race against race and by preaching the superiority of what it calls "Aryans." In general throughout the history of the western Christian world we find, both under Catholic feudalism and Protestant capitalism, attitudes ranging from distrust to ill-concealed contempt for science. Much philosophy has been, therefore, a means of reconciling science and religion and of keeping the former in a carefully limited place. The ways of doing this will be discussed in later chapters, but they consist in general of finding that science deals only with what are called the appearances of things while religion alone can penetrate to the higher reality. Those who have no outworn institutions to maintain, who do not profit by the existing order of things, might well ask what it is these people want to conceal concerning the nature of the world and man. Why must it be so stoutly maintained that there is a *truth* above and apart from the *truths* actually discovered through careful experimentation with things?

Chapter four on the philosophy of science will attempt to present and analyze some of the more important philosophical interpretations of science and especially the relationship of science and modern materialism. It is sufficient now to indicate how philosophy began as general speculation about the universe and then how, as special bodies of knowledge developed, it branched out into the various sciences. This early created the problem of the relation of the parent stream to its increasingly numerous offspring and relations by marriage, as it were. One result was the narrowing of philosophy to what came to be called metaphysics, or the study of first principles, supposed to be above and apart from the subject matter of special sciences, and regarded as a body of eternal truths. Another result was the gradual development of philosophies or, as they may be called, theories of special subjects, such as the philosophy of physics, the philosophy of art, mental philosophy (which has given way to the science of psychology), and so on. In this sense philosophy means the theory of something as opposed to its practice, or the more general and abstract features of a subject as opposed to its more limited and specific aspects. It is important that there be such theories, but they involve dangers when there is such a division of labor that different people perform these essentially inseparable tasks. This paves the way further for a conception of philosophy as the theory of theory, which is equal to just pure theory or the theory of nothing in particular. At least one of the reasons philosophy tends so much in this direction is because philosophers, as members of the dominant social and economic class which must find a justification for its existence, cannot do so under contemporary conditions of capitalist society without turning away from the concrete world of social facts around them. The early philosophers of the rising middle class in the seventeenth and eighteenth centuries had real practical problems confronting them—many of which centered around that of providing theoretical justification for modern bourgeois institutions as opposed to those of a feudal society they were designed to replace. Today the international working-class movement, for example, has its own philosophy, which it uses as an instrument for the criticism of the institutions and theoretical justifications of capitalism, and as the basis of the new theory and practice of socialism.

This raises the question of the goal or aim of philosophy. Every different type of philosophy has had its own conception of what the purpose of philosophy is. It will be worth our while to survey briefly some of the most important and divergent aims. When ancient philosophy was taken over by Christianity it was described as "the handmaiden of theology." In this tradition its purpose was to uphold and buttress the structure of Christian beliefs, and to this end it has been predominantly used down to our own day. So-called revealed truth, as found in the Bible, took precedence over all rational and scientific inquiry. Of course, this purpose has often not been expressed openly and is frequently diluted. Orthodox Christianity is thinned out, but the purpose of most philosophy is still to uphold an essentially religious attitude towards the world. One good expression of this is found in the motto of a philosophical magazine published in St. Louis some fifty years ago: "Philosophy bakes no bread but it gives us God, Freedom, and Immortality." To sum up, from this standpoint the purpose of philosophy is to find a justification for the existing religious attitude towards the world, the major features of which are not to be questioned.

For the Greeks, philosophy was intended primarily to provide a rational basis for a desired mode of life. Epicurus, for example, sought peace and the avoidance of pain, sought a refuge from the troubles of the world around him and a guarantee that there would be no future life to plague him. He formulated a conception of the world that would give him his desired tranquillity. Philosophy for him and his school thus became a way of thinking that would eliminate the supernatural and help men to rely upon themselves for the attainment of a rational and happy life. The Stoics thought the world was harsh and often cruel but that it must exist through some divine plan and for some reason. Therefore, they taught that all men should do their duty, and perform, faithfully and without complaining, the part assigned to them in this life. Yet, because of its emphasis on reason as inherent in the world and in all men, Stoicism tended towards a humanitarianism which transcended narrow racial and nationalistic boundaries.

Plato, whatever his "pure" theoretical interests may have been, used philosophy to justify the life of leisure of the Greek land-owning aristocracy and to uphold the ideal of an oligarchic state ruled over by an *élite* to whom alone affairs of state can be safely entrusted. The aim and purpose of life for Plato was simply to know, and it is the function of those who are not in a position to cultivate knowledge to labor for those who are. This knowing was not knowledge as we conceive it today. It was not knowledge of particular things such as underlies all our sciences. Such knowledge belongs to the artisan, the workers, who do things with their hands. Real knowing consists in contemplation of what were supposed by Plato to be the eternal forms of things, not a particular beautiful object, for example, or the actual means of making a beautiful statue or building, but a supposed pure or abstract beauty. Just what beauty is that is not the beauty of a particular person or thing has never been made clear, but Plato in like manner sought the contemplation of an equally abstract justice, truth, and goodness. Plato's tendency is not so much to make philosophy serve social well-being, but to impose a social order that there may be philosophers at the top of the pyramid of social classes. Plato came from a well-to-do land-owning family that found itself suffering from the rise of a new commercial and manufacturing class, and many of the features of his philosophy can be ascribed to the desire of his class to keep the old order of things, to keep strictly defined classes and to avoid change.

Aristotle, who was the greatest of the Greek philosophers, had a somewhat different social position. His family lived at the court of Philip of Macedonia to whom his father was a physician, and he came under the influence of the idea of a vast Macedonian Empire that would embrace the whole eastern world. Thus he had a broader social perspective and his philosophy dif-

fers from that of Plato in being more interested in particular fields of knowledge, more concerned with
knowing the actual world around him. But he could
only conceive society on a slave basis, and this consideration seems to have influenced much of Aristotle's
thought concerning human beings. In his Ethics, he
develops his ideal of human life. It is an ethics for the
rich man, denying in fact that the poor man can ever
be virtuous, and of course not considering slaves at all.
Again, as with Plato, the purpose of all human society
is that a few might live lives of leisure and wealth, supposedly then to engage in the highest of all activities—
the pure knowing of the first principles of the universe.

This analysis is of course over-simplified. The forces
and influences acting on any man are indefinitely complicated. But it can be maintained that this mode of
approach does provide clues to the understanding of
philosophers that no other approach can provide. It has
long been a commonplace that a thinker is the product
of his age. All that is being maintained here is that such
a doctrine is much too broad: a thinker is the product
of *his* position in an age, or in other words, of the
particular complex of social forces that impinge upon
him.

Throughout much recent philosophy, with the exception of the pragmatists, whose leader is John Dewey,
who have fallen into the swamp of relativism and subjectivism, emphasis is placed again on pure contemplation. A well known philosopher was recently heard to
say that he thought it "indecent" for philosophers to

consider such paltry things as men and their social life. The remark was made in the interests of the "purity" of philosophy, in behalf of speculation on abstract questions of metaphysics. This divorce of philosophy from all the pressing problems of contemporary science and social life is supposed to indicate the nobility of the philosophical profession, its superiority to all that is transient, earthly, human. Rather does it attest the decline and bankruptcy of the Platonic philosophical tradition.

During the early centuries of the development of modern science and at recurring periods since, some philosophers sought to perform the important task of interpreting this new science, of trying to get fuller and more complete understanding of the world through man's growing scientific knowledge. This was, as has been suggested earlier, connected with the fact that the growth of science and technology was necessary for the rising manufacturing and commercial class. Furthermore, as this class grew in power it met the opposition of the established feudal order. This provided its theoreticians with an additional and very practical task, namely, that of providing a sound basis of criticism of existing feudal institutions. In this sense philosophy became revolutionary. John Locke, the leading theoretician of the bourgeois revolution in England in the latter part of the seventeenth century, was led, by the new developments in science and the political conflicts of his time, to make a whole new analysis of how we get knowledge and of how we can test its certainty. He did this in order to clear away such hindering notions as that man's mind contains in itself certain true ideas which require no verification by experience. His method had the further advantage of dispensing with the notion of the divine right of kings and of putting political questions in general on a purely rational basis.

The English revolution represented, however, a unique system of compromises and thus we must turn to eighteenth-century France for a clearer view of philosophy in its progressive social role. There we find an amazingly ingenious and energetic body of thinkers, intellectuals who were the vanguard of their social class, struggling against the hampering conditions imposed upon them by monarchical, priest-ridden France. The striking thing about these men is that they all embraced materialism, in whole or in part. This meant to them primarily that men are the products of their environment and therefore that any demand for human improvement must be a demand for better social institutions, for a better environment. Their aim was human happiness, they stated, and this required man's knowledge of himself and of nature. The greatest hindrance to human progress, they thought, was the corrupting force of religion with all its paraphernalia of superstition, priest, and sacrament. We can see today that this attack upon religion was motivated in part by the hold the church had on political, economic, and social life, and that the shortcoming of these philosophers was their failure to analyze political institutions and social forces as the expression of the economic processes of society. By economic process is meant here simply the ways in which men get their living and the resultant system of human relationships involved in the production and distribution of the means of human existence. This whole philosophical movement found its expression in the slogan "Liberty, Equality, Fraternity" of the French Revolution. Having attained their end, political power, the French bourgeoisie dropped off "fraternity" and made liberty and equality stand for abstract equality before the law and the liberty of men with money to engage in industry and commerce as they desired. But with all its shortcomings, this materialist philosophy of eighteenth-century France was the nearest approach mankind had yet made to a philosophy for the masses of people, a completely rational philosophy whose sole aim was the advancement of general human well-being. It is interesting to note that this philosophy was taken up in America by a group of men, among whom was Thomas Jefferson, who feared the growing might of the Federalists led by Alexander Hamilton and who sought a return to the democratic principles of the American Revolution.

It is to Germany we must turn for the further development of this phase of philosophy. There, after long practical and theoretical turmoil, inspired in large part by the repercussions of the French Revolution upon men enmeshed in feudal institutions, appeared the writings of the philosopher Hegel. The current conflict of class forces introduced conflicting elements into Hegel's philosophy and led his disciples after his death to split up into violently opposed groups. This was due for the most part to the fact that Hegel sought to combine a revolutionary theory of change with the glorification of Protestant Christianity and the Prussian state; and, while an advocate of the new bourgeois order, was willing to make many compromises with the old regime. Looked at more technically, Hegel combined a dynamic interpretation of human thought and action with the idea derived from Plato of an eternal system of ideas or principles, manifested in the world of nature and man, which he called the *absolute idea*. The first aspect of his philosophy is referred to as dialectics, the second as idealism. Thus with one hand Hegel offered a dynamic universe, developing in time, phase succeeding phase in a widening spiral, and with the other he took this away and gave an Absolute (another name for God) which was fixed and timeless. While the first implied that man, by knowledge of the laws of development of society, could and should direct and control social change, the second, by his endowing existing institutions with the blessing of the Absolute, implied that all was well and should be left as it is. Thus Hegel, having advanced greatly beyond the French materialists by developing the active creative aspect of human thought and the dynamic process of society, was stopped short by his contentment with the compromises of the existing order and its reflection, in his thought, in the form of the Absolute.

Among those who gathered at the University of Berlin and studied philosophy after Hegel's death was a young German, Karl Marx. After much theoretical struggle Marx became a "Hegelian," but soon found it impossible to reconcile Hegel's idealism, which culminated in the adoration of a constitutional monarchy, with the actual situation in Germany. Led into active political work Marx always took the side of the oppressed and the downtrodden. This brought him into conflict with the police and sent him into exile. He made the acquaintance of another German student, Frederick Engels, who emphasized the need for knowing the work that had been done by English economists (for Engels had lived in England) in order to understand the social and political problems of their day. Thus Marx, through his own practical political experience, through his study of and participation in the struggles of the working class, through his knowledge of French utopian socialism and his mastery of English political economy, and with his philosophical training, was led to transform Hegel's theory of change, together with the materialist teachings of the eighteenth-century French philosophers, into a new and revolutionary philosophy that came to be known as dialectical materialism. He was aided in this by the work of Ludwig Feuerbach, a student of Hegel's, who rebelled against his master's idealism and turned back to Spinoza in combination with the teachings of the French materialists. Feuerbach helped to lead Marx to materialism, but Marx thought he had mistakenly rejected the dialectics along with the idealism of Hegel instead of transforming it materialistically. He saw the limitations of

Feuerbach's materialism and criticized it in a series of eleven important notes. Most important among these were the criticism of the older materialism's notion of sensation as something passive and subjective instead of as a practical human activity, and the notion that men are products of circumstances and upbringing which failed to recognize that "circumstances are changed precisely by men and that the educator must himself be educated."

Marx was led likewise, simultaneously, and by the same forces, to transform utopian into scientific socialism. Marx and Engels thought and wrote on many subjects, producing volumes upon volumes on political economy, history and philosophy. But underlying all their works is their philosophy of dialectical materialism —a philosophy consisting of two essential and inseparable elements: a strictly materialistic conception of the universe, and the dialectical conception of the nature of all movement and process, together with a technique of analyzing actual complexes of developing forces.

Since, in this chapter, we are concerned primarily with the social status and function of philosophies, it is necessary to look at dialectical materialism from the standpoint of its class basis and its social purpose. We have seen that the earlier philosophies represented the world as it appeared in the light of the needs and interests of particular social groups. This is equally true of dialectical materialism, except that here, for the first time, instead of its being concealed and glossed over, it is recognized and explicitly asserted. This is so because it is the philosophy of the working class which, unlike all previous classes struggling to rule society, has nothing to conceal since it does not seek to become a new exploiting class but rather to abolish all exploitation of man by man, and to destroy thereby the division of society into social and economic classes. Nor is dialectical materialism any the less true because it is a class philosophy. To say this would be to deny that there is any truth in any of the previous philosophies. It is just because the working class, whether building a socialist society in the U.S.S.R. or struggling for better conditions and ultimately for socialism in other lands, is the progressive force in the contemporary world, that it carries with it the greatest intellectual and cultural achievements of the past and requires a sound and true philosophy as a basis for all its struggles. Furthermore, just as the proletariat seeks the socialist reconstruction of society not for the perpetuation of itself as a class but in order to abolish all classes, so dialectical materialism, as the philosophy of this class, is not something narrowly partisan and hence only relatively true at best, but is objectively true as the philosophy of all progressive humanity.

For Marx and Engels philosophy had a great and important task to perform, that of directing men to such knowledge of themselves, society, and of the physical world as would bring about the fullest possible development of all human beings. They saw that philosophy, to be meaningful, had actually to concern itself with the real needs and desires of the masses of men, together with the scientific knowledge of nature and society by which alone these desires could be realized in fact. Under the conditions of capitalist society this required a philosophy of and for the working class—a philosophy and a science which would enable the proletariat to struggle successfully for the improvement of its conditions and through these struggles eventually to win political power and put an end to its own exploitation by liberating all society from the fetters of capitalist economy. But philosophy, in seeking these aims, ceased to be philosophy at all in the traditional sense. In fact, Engels pointed out that with the development of modern or dialectical materialism all that remained of former philosophy is the science of thought and its laws. All else is merged in the positive sciences of nature and history. In other words, this new materialism no longer needs any philosophy standing above the sciences. Philosophy thus became for Marx and Engels not a mere theory but the actual expression of the demand for a better life and the knowledge required for its attainment. This is where all previous philosophies had erred. "Philosophers have only interpreted the world differently," Marx said, "the point is to change it."

II. MATERIALISM
AND IDEALISM

NATURE OR GOD — CONFLICTING ATTITUDES TOWARDS EVIL — EARTH AND HEAVEN — PIE IN THE SKY — APPEARANCE AND REALITY — BERKELEY'S DENIAL OF MATTER — FUNCTIONS OF THE IDEA OF GOD — IDEALISM AND SOCIAL CONSERVATISM — THE PURPOSE AND MEANING OF PRAYER — MATERIALISM — BASIC PRINCIPLES OF MATERIALISM — MATERIALISM AS A THEORY OF SOCIETY AND HISTORY — THE MATERIALIST WAY OF LIFE

"ONLY the Almighty can answer why these have fallen victims to the flames," declared the minister, his gaze sweeping the five pine coffins of the Spellman family, burned to death in their tenement house on the East Side of New York in 1934. "Where is thy mercy? Only he who dwells in the high heaven knows the secrets of life." Thus was the tragic destruction of a whole family of five, coming as it did in an endless series of disastrous tenement house fires, referred to the inscrutable will of an almighty God. Others, apparently, thought differently, for in response to the same tragedy they formed neighborhood organizations to demand action on the part of the city officials: enforcement of the fire regulations that had long been in abeyance in New York's old-law tenements and a genuine low cost housing program. These two reactions reveal the difference between two fundamental points of view, two philosophies: idealism and materialism. The term idealism is used here in its broadest meaning to include all forms of religion as well as idealistic philosophies which are simply more subtle and more highly rarefied forms of religious conceptions of the world.

Minister, priest, rabbi, idealist philosopher:—they frequently tend to have a common way of viewing the world and man. Over and above nature stands God, spirit, mind or, as the philosophers like to call it, the Absolute. Everything that happens is part of a divine plan, and although many things may seem evil to our limited point of view, all is really for the best. It matters little if one says with the Moslem that all is fated by the will of Allah, with the Christian that all things are guided by God's providence, with Leibniz that this is the best of all possible worlds, or if one agrees with Hegel that whatever is real is rational. These are expressions of one idea, the idea that all is really for the best and that it is not for us weak and puny mortals to scrutinize the divine plan of the world or to take affairs into our own hands. Shall men chastise the unjust? "Vengeance is mine, saith the Lord." Shall the oppressed peoples of the Roman Empire pay tribute for their privilege of being slaves? "Render unto Caesar the things that are Caesar's and unto God the things that are God's." Shall the long down-trodden Irish tear themselves free from English imperialism? "The meek shall inherit the earth." Shall fire-traps be destroyed and decent homes built for men and women? "Who can fathom thy inscrutable ways, O God?"

The clergyman, then, who bowed his head in awe before God and the bodies of these five persons, was merely being true to an ancient and highly respectable tradition. If a perfect and all powerful deity created the world and all that it contains, then it must be good, and evil must only appear to be so to our benighted eyes. Or, as an American philosopher, Josiah Royce, put it, "The very presence of ill in the temporal order is the condition of the perfection of the eternal order." The idealist may not see that in taking this position he is accepting and upholding human society as it happens to exist at any given time and is denying to men the right or the power to improve their conditions. To be an idealist means to seek in the will of a God or the eternal order of a World Spirit the explanation of the varying fortunes of men. To be a materialist means to look for the actual, material, conditions and causes of things in order that men by knowing the world around them can live better.

One of the motives that has caused men to believe in a God and has upheld that belief is the desire for immortality. The process whereby men came to believe in a future life, a life after Death, is unimportant to us now. In the history of Western civilization several reasons for this desire are clear. Life has on the whole not been happy for the masses of men. Poverty, insecurity, and distress have been the rule for most of mankind. Ever recurrent famines and pestilences have added to human misery. Men aspired to so much and attained so little. What was it worth, this brief span of incessant toil and much suffering between birth and the grave? Surely it was not for this that men have come into being! So they have pictured for themselves a heaven, another and better world for which the present one is but a trial and a preparation. And if this life was bad, men made it worse that the future life might be better. In heaven were pictured to be the things that this life so sorely lacked. For the Moslem in the desert the Koran pictures a heaven with running brooks and pleasant shade. For the American Indian it was a Happy Hunting Ground, abounding in game and free from the depredations of the white man. The story is told of a Jesuit priest who failed to convert a group of Eskimos to Christianity because he could not honestly promise them that there were seals in heaven. Choirs of white robed angels singing eternally in praise of God scarcely made up in the minds of these practical men for the absence of the seal, the means of their subsistence.

A far more subtle conception of this spiritual realm or Heaven is found in the thought of the German philosopher Fichte. For him the spiritual world is a realm in which, unlike the material world we live in, our desires are realized, our purposes cannot miscarry, and where to will something is *ipso facto* to attain it. Obviously Fichte, his desire for a nobler humanity thwarted by the Germany of his time, finds in this idea of a spiritual world just that guarantee of the realization of his desires he cannot accomplish in this one. This further illustrates how the traditional Christian conception of Heaven and the etherialized spiritual world of the idealist philosophers serve the same general purpose. The "Pie in the Sky" motif of the famous I. W. W. song is common to both.

But Heaven serves other purposes. God must surely be a just God. Yet on earth there is much injustice. The poor man who leads a hard and frugal life sees those who are wicked and prodigal of the fruits of his labor enjoying all the good things of this world. There is no justice on earth! Surely there must be another life where the sinful, the exploiters, will suffer for their brief happiness on earth, while those who have toiled here will reap their reward. Lazarus the beggar, so the story told by Jesus goes, took up his place outside a rich man's gate, desiring to be fed with the crumbs that fell from his table. But the day came when the beggar and the rich man died. The former was taken to Heaven into the bosom of Abraham. The latter suffered the fires of Hell. And the rich man seeing Lazarus in Heaven asked Abraham to send him down with water to quench his awful thirst. But Abraham replied, "Son, remember that thou in thy life time receivedst thy good things, and likewise Lazarus evil things: but now he is comforted, and thou art tormented." This idea of punishment and reward for nothing but former pleasure and misery would constitute a happily poetic beggar's justice were it not so purely fictitious. Workers have been urged by misleaders not to strike, not to act against their exploiters and to seek better conditions, because of this same attitude generally inculcated by the church. If we are meek and patient, they say, God will reward us and in Hell our exploiters will be punished for their sins. The materialist revolt against this view was eloquently expressed a century ago by the German poet and revolutionary, Heinrich Heine, when he declared, "Men can no longer be put off with promissory notes upon heaven. They now claim as their inalienable right the enjoyment of this earth."

There are today in the churches, movements and groups which, composed of those with a higher degree of social consciousness, are like Heine not satisfied with the promise that in Heaven the Kingdom of God will prevail. These seek to make it prevail on earth, often against the opposition of higher authorities in the churches. Various Protestant denominations, reformed Jewish sects, and movements within the Catholic Church are working for a larger measure of social justice and for the fulfillment of certain broad social ideals. It is noteworthy that the Nazis find even the Christian religion with its professed ideal of human brotherhood, albeit in the abstract, too progressive for their reactionary and anti-scientific race theories. Although religion has helped to keep alive before men certain ideals of value in human social life, these ideals unless fertilized by definitely materialistic or "this-worldly" impulses often prove a drawback to progress. It is to be kept in mind that our purpose here is not to analyze organized religion as a social institution but to inquire into the way spiritualistic ideas function in social life.

Philosophers do not always accept the religious teaching of a heaven and hell. But from Plato to the present day many have found a way of accomplishing a similar result. They do this by one or another form of idealism. The fundamental principle of idealism is that matter, the actual material world we find ourselves a part of, is not the final reality. To the idealist the physical world is not really what it is to us: that is, existing by itself, changing its form but neither arising nor passing away. For what is real we must look elsewhere since matter is only the reflection, the appearance of something beyond. This other thing, this reality as it is called, is of the nature of reason, mind, or spirit. This is what is real, what is self-existing, and matter is but its reflection or appearance. Now it is not hard, except for some professional philosophers, to see that this is merely another version, a more subtle account of the beliefs of religion. The result is the same. The actual world of nature is made to appear trivial and unimportant, a mere "appearance." Beyond it is "Reality"— an intelligent and perfect system. In short, while the world may appear to be without direction or purpose, in reality, it is a spiritual order guided towards its destiny by a divine plan. Furthermore, the whole body of concrete knowledge which we call science stands condemned as dealing only with "appearance," while faith, pure reason, intuition, or just sheer "immediate experience" grasp "reality."

For some philosophers the whole universe is but an idea, or system of ideas, in the mind of God. For others it is God himself, and for still others it is just Spirit or Reason. Matter, in any case, is something inferior and subordinate. This is to say, primarily, that there are no such things as material causes, that mind or spirit is alone the cause of everything. This means that our ideas are not caused by material things but rather material things exist only in our ideas. For society it means that the environment does not make men what they are, cause them to have all the ideas and purposes they have, but that men make their environment out of whole cloth (their ideas).

The mechanical materialism of the eighteenth century could only assert that men are products of their environment. Against this the idealists maintained the opposite, equally one-sided, that the environment is made by men. Dialectical materialism, as will be shown, recognized the limitations of both these views, showing that men and their environment, natural and social, are in constant interaction, that men have made their social institutions, their cities, etc., but have made them as a result of previous conditions and experience and are in turn re-made by these objective results of their own activity. The mechanical materialists made it appear impossible that men by knowledge and thought could change their environment. The idealists made it appear that pure ideas and inner urges did not arise from actual conditions but were the result of the functioning of pure spirit, and secondly, that these ideas themselves had that propelling force which brought about their realization in the actual world.

George Berkeley, who became a Bishop of the Church of England, is the most interesting and best known modern advocate of idealist views. He stated clearly that it was the belief in the existence of matter that caused irreligion and atheism. He was determined, therefore, to destroy this belief in order that men would have to believe in a God as the creator of all that is. To him it was a question of either matter or God and he chose to do away with matter. But his own writings show that matter was not so easy to dispose of. He argued that things exist only in so far as they are seen or perceived by us, or, in other words, that nothing exists except as my mind, your mind, or some other mind perceives it. He was able to argue this with some plausibility by reducing every possible material object, including our own bodies, to a collection of sensations, such as redness, hardness, heaviness, and so on in some being's mind. When the difficult problem arose of the existence of things that no one now perceives or which hadn't yet been discovered, such as the North Pole, or distant stars, he resorted to the notion that God perceives them. But it remained clear that he had less basis for assuming the existence of God than the materialist has for believing in the material world. Nevertheless, Berkeley's philosophy created a considerable stir in the intellectual world because it provided an argument for those men who wanted to keep things just as they were. Whatever we experience in nature and society are the ideas that God gives us and surely we should not try to change God! Having free will men can make ideas for themselves, but that is just how evil arises. But Berkeley's theory was soon felt to be weak and much of the history of philosophy from his time to the present has consisted in attempts to revise his philosophy and to put it on a firmer basis or simply to dress up the same thing in better clothing.

The philosophy of Berkeley gives us an excellent insight into the relation between a system of philosophy and the actual way people think about their ordinary problems. To most people the statement that all the things of the world around us, the earth and sun and stars, the houses we live in, the tools we handle, our bodies and the food with which we feed our bodies, are *ideas* indeed sounds very strange. Berkeley admitted this himself, writing, "But after all, say you, it sounds very harsh to say we eat and drink ideas, and are clothed with ideas." He answers that this isn't nearly as difficult to accept as is the view that things can exist that are not perceived by any mind. Now to most of us it is perfectly easy to believe that the house we live in or the place in which we work, or the North Pole, or Halley's Comet, exist quite as well in our absence as in our presence. We do not believe that our minds have anything to do with *making* these things, or causing them to come into existence. We believe likewise that the earth and the rest of the solar system were here before there were men to know them. Now Berkeley believes the very same thing. He is often incorrectly criticized for denying that these things exist. In general idealism has been much misunderstood. This is a serious matter for those who wish to think correctly, for unless we clearly understand what the idealist is doing we may ourselves fall into idealistic ways of thinking without knowing it. It was for this reason that Lenin wrote a whole volume against a particular modern form of idealism that Otto Bauer and other so-called Marxists were teaching to the Austrian workers. If idealism is thought of as something so ridiculous that no one in his right mind can believe it, then we do not understand why it has played such a tremendous role in all modern thought and is so steadily taught to this day.

What, therefore, did Berkeley mean and what does idealism in general mean? Berkeley himself said that he sought to destroy materialism as the belief in the existence of a physical world independent from God, because in doing so he would be taking the ground out from under the atheist's feet (both figuratively and literally). Once material objects, in short, a universe, is allowed to exist apart from relation to any mind, then the existence of God becomes difficult if not impossible to demonstrate and might as well be dispensed with. Therefore, Berkeley's argument seems to go: matter must be shown to be dependent on its being known, so that God can be retained as the supreme knower, or as that mind for which the whole universe exists as opposed to our minds for which only fragments exist. We are thus brought back to the old question: What is God? And this is less a question of what God is defined to be than of the purpose in the world God is thought of as fulfilling.

The primary purposes of God are, first, to provide a convenient explanation for whatever happens to be— floods, famine, poverty, class distinctions, war, etc. They are because God willed them, and God must have willed them for a purpose. Here we see the type of reasoning illustrated at the beginning of this chapter. Or we can take innumerable other examples. Several years ago Reverend Tytheridge, preaching at high mass in St. Patrick's cathedral in New York, said that the trials most of us are suffering in the form of poverty or economic stress should not be regarded as manifestations of God's indifference but as an opportunity to share in the sufferings He visits upon those He loves. Tens of thousands of sermons have been preached in America alone since the crisis began in 1929 *"proving"* that the crisis came from God and that it came for a *good purpose.*

A second purpose God fulfills is in explaining anything we are unable at a given time to explain otherwise. The multitude of animal species, for example, seemed utterly inexplicable to our forefathers, before Darwin, except that God wanted to express his power and glory in as many ways as possible. In the same way, God "explained" every sort of natural phenomenon that science had not yet discovered the answer to: the evolution of man, the change of the seasons, birth and death, life itself, and, in fact, the reason why there was a universe at all. To this last question science does not even pretend to give an answer. It doesn't believe that the question has any meaning, unless, indeed we have already proved that a God exists, in reference to whom such meaning would be found.

But the third and most important function that God is used to serve is that of providing some kind of meaning, reason, or purpose for human life. This is necessary, of course, only because in most conditions under which human life *has* been lived there has been so little purpose. The question, what is the purpose of life, is asked only when life has no purpose. "Surely," the oppressed cry, "it was not for this that we were created." And the convenient answer is found that this life is but a preparation for the life to come, a sort of proving ground through which God selects those He shall take unto Himself after death. The idea of God thus justifies whatever is, by finding its meaning and justification elsewhere. It is for these reasons that Marx said: "Religion is the moan of the oppressed creature, the sentiment of a heartless world, as it is the spirit of spiritless conditions. It is the opium of the people."

It is not our purpose here to take up the more personal side of religious belief, its more subjective aspects of providing consolation for the death of loved ones, or confidence in pursuing a path which is believed to have been consecrated by a higher power which is working for and with men. These aspects of religion exist and are real, but history and contemporary experience reveal that men can find similar consolation without belief in God. Besides, it is the more objective or social consequences of religion that here concern us.

It is not to be overlooked that religion has often served progressive social purposes. Through religious ideas the struggling tribes of Israel were brought together as a unified people and, as Marx and Engels discussed at length in their correspondence, religious doctrines enabled Mohammed to weld the long suffering Arabs into a powerful nation. Likewise it was the monk Martin Luther who led the great mass revolt against Catholic feudalism which created conditions favorable to the development of modern commerce and industry, and it was the Calvinist Puritans who, inspired by religious ideas, struggled in New England against almost insuperable odds for the realization of their ideal of a kingdom of righteousness on this continent. Similarly, today, there are many devoutly religious people working for the new socialist society in the U. S. S. R., fighting for the democratic people's government in Spain, and struggling on behalf of the exploited in other countries of the world. Catholic, Protestant, and Jew are in the same picket lines as are non-believers, and there are clergymen of all sects who stand forth valiantly against reaction in America as many stand against Hitler's fascism in Germany itself. These men are motivated in their defense of human rights by the ideals and convictions of their religion. Father Michael O'Flanagan sincerely believes that, "Today, Russia is doing the work of God in China and in Spain," and he gives profound expression to the noblest elements of religious faith when he says, as he did in this country in 1938, "I believe that the real God who rules the universe will smile upon the people in Russia who are doing His will, even though they have been shocked into infidelity by the evil deeds that were done in His name, rather than upon those who prate about His name in order to cover up the iniquity of their actions."

The moral of this is that spiritualistic ideas and attitudes are not in and of themselves either progressive or reactionary. They may be used for either purpose, depending upon the way they are applied to social problems and the other ideas with which they come to be associated. They are not, however, dependable, and cannot serve in our age as the basis of the world working-class struggle for socialism. This is true in spite of the fact that not only is there no necessary incompatibility between religion and the practical objectives of socialism but, on the contrary, in so far as religion teaches the brotherhood of man and the intrinsic dignity and value of each human being, it requires socialism for the realization of these ideals. What happens too often, unfortunately, is that considerations of the "other world" interfere with our needs and desires in this one, and that abstract and reputedly divine principles can so easily be invoked as arguments for passivity and against precisely those actions necessary today for the achievement of a better society.

It is more imperative now tnan ever that religious differences not be allowed to interfere, either among the various sects or denominations or between religious and non-religious people, with united social action on behalf of those ideals held in common by all progressives. Some few years ago a layman's commission, headed by Professor Hocking of Harvard's Philosophy Department, and financed largely by John D. Rockefeller Jr., after studying Christian missionary work in the eastern world urged that Christianity make common cause with Mohammedanism, Buddhism and other religions in combating the growing forces of materialism, especially as represented by the philosophies of Marx and Lenin. Ostensibly, this "united front" is proposed for the purpose of defending religion, but it might well have been conceived as a crusade in defense of the economic and political *status quo* against socialism, since the theory and practice of socialism is the beginning and end of the philosophy of Marx and Lenin. Precisely here is the great issue before religious people today—shall they unite on what are supposedly religious grounds against the struggle for greater democracy and socialism, or shall they unite with all social progressives against the forces of reaction and fascism? It is especially noteworthy that the spheres of Christian missions and of imperialist colonial domination are virtually identical and that therefore Professor Hocking's call serves nicely the interests of the imperialist states and their economic rulers.

Returning to Berkeley and philosophical idealism, we can now say that its purpose is to continue spiritualist lines of thought and to maintain spiritualist attitudes towards the world and human life. Either this world exists as part of a divine scheme of things—all that occurs is directed by a God or Gods for the attainment of some divine end, and man must seek not his material or earthly well-being but heavenly awards—or the universe exists in and of itself, events occur through natural causes, many of which can be changed by human action based on knowledge of causal relations, and man's sole possible goal or end is the greatest degree of human well-being possible. In short, we have either idealism or materialism. Just as idealism means, in the last analysis, the reference of all events to some sort of God or Universal Spirit, and the purpose of human life to a realm beyond, materialism means the explanation of all that occurs by actual events and processes in the natural and social world around us, and the search for that knowledge of things and power over them necessary to satisfy men's wants and desires. If this be true it is not surprising that we so often find idealism on the side of preserving existing social institutions and conditions, and materialism on the side of criticism and the attempt to change what exists. With certain notable exceptions, this has proved to be the case, especially when we look beyond individual philosophers to the larger movements in philosophical thought.

It has frequently been said that materialism is a philosophy of young men and idealism of old. While this belief hits upon something important, namely, that the young in general are seeking to make a place for themselves in the world, and the old to keep the place they hold, it is far less true and less significant than the recognition that idealism is pre-eminently the philosophy of a social class that is striving to maintain its dominance, and materialism that of a rising social class that aims to overthrow the old and establish a new order. Today this is especially evident in the struggle between dialectical materialism and the various forms of idealism, and as is to be expected in all such theoretical conflicts as in practical ones, there are those who seek to escape both sides by finding some neutral ground on which they can stand. The philosophy known as logical positivism is a good example of this "liberal" attempt to avoid facing the issues before us. It is to be noted that mechanistic materialism, which has at times been used to justify given institutions by brutally accepting existing oppression and inequality, has, since Marx and Engels formulated dialectical materialism, tended more and more to be an ally in the idealist camp by its crude, over-simplified formulations.

It is impossible to overestimate the importance of spiritualism or idealism as a potential instrument of social conservatism and often of reaction. Developed and elaborated into religious or philosophical systems, it is but the crystallization of a whole set of attitudes towards the problems of life and a codification of the ways of reacting to concrete situations. Its difference from materialism is seen in opposite approaches to questions which confront us. The unity of the idealist and spiritualist positions is often lost in the many different ways they have of handling questions. Let us take war as an ex-

ample. Such a catastrophe as the World War was justified from these points of view in innumerable ways that
yet come to one and the same thing. It was said to be
caused by man's pugnacious instinct—it is human nature
to fight. This argument is especially confusing because it
may seem to many people to be "naturalistic," that is,
an explanation by reference to nature. But we have
already seen that idealism regards the events in which
man is involved as flowing out of him or as directed
by a World-Spirit, and never regards man as a product
of events. Here it is clear that human nature is viewed
as something absolute, something "given" once and for
all, and whatever man does flows from what he eternally
is. Another common explanation of such an event as the
World War is that it was caused by human greed and
selfishness. This is like the preceding argument, but it
has the additional implication that if only men's hearts
were changed there would not be war. And how are
men's hearts changed? The answer is always that we
need more religious education, that religion alone can
make men generous and altruistic. This is based on the
theory that man is "by nature" bad and what good he is
capable of comes only from God.

Another important idealist approach is the one, fa-
miliar to us now, that although war *seems* evil it must
really be good and have come about for some divine
purpose. This is perfectly logical when one starts with
the assumption that the world is God's creation and all
its events the manifestation of his will. We may even
write the history of the World War as Hegel wrote his-

tory until his day "so that the ill that is found in the World may be comprehended, and the thinking Spirit reconciled with the fact of the existence of evil." But it brings men to wonder at the devious ways in which God accomplishes his purpose and to scorn the pious "Amen" which may punctuate any catastrophe, natural or social.

Putting together these approaches to the question of war, one striking similarity stands out. None of them either makes, or encourages the making of, an actual concrete analysis of just how the World War came about, what factors promoted it, whose interests were being served in the various belligerent countries, and so on. To ask those questions and to explore war or any other social happening in that manner is to take a materialist rather than an idealist approach, as the idealists themselves have not been slow to recognize. The World War is only an illustration of an attitude towards all other pressing problems. It is easy to apply these same approaches to the questions of poverty, unemployment, economic crises, crime, and all other human ills.

The chief, and often only remedy that spiritualism has to offer is that of prayer. There is nothing in the world that men can desire that they are not urged to seek by the method of prayer. Men pray for health and long life, for rain and prosperity, for peace and progress. We find even the anomaly of Liberty League pastors leading their congregations in prayer that God may guide President Roosevelt in the path of truth and

righteousness, that is, to acceptance of the policies of
the giant monopolies. Underlying prayer are the suppo-
sitions that there is a wise, good, and powerful God;
that He listens to our expressed desires; and that He
thereby may be moved to change the course of events.
But therein lies a serious contradiction. All that happens is in accordance with the divine plan, yet we ask
God to change this plan when it is not agreeable with
our desires. When the Pope prayed for the cessation of
war in Ethiopia he surely must have thought that the
war could not have come about in the first place unless
it had been God's will. Secondly, laying that difficulty
aside, we must ask just how God was to intervene. It
was not clear whether he was to bring Britain and the
other world powers in on the side of Haile Selassie to
stop Italy, or to soften the heart of Mussolini and have
him withdraw his troops, or to make Ethiopia lay down
its arms and surrender to the invading Italians.

The question of the efficacy of prayer is hardly worth
raising. The real point is that prayer is a most effective
way *of doing nothing to change existing conditions.*
This is strikingly illustrated by a sermon preached in
New York last January by the Reverend Henry Sloane
Coffin. Dr. Coffin declared that many are gloomy at the
prospects of another world war, and added: "But if we
are believers in God the last word must always be of
hope in Him. What does such hope mean? It means
that in any situation He has a purpose for us, and a
purpose in which He wishes us to work. At this hour
in the world's affairs it is surely God's will that we hope

and pray for peace and do not supinely declare that war is inevitable. . . ." Besides the glaring contradiction here between God's having a purpose for us in any situation and our praying that what he might bring about should not come to pass, it is obvious that if war comes it is God's purpose and we should find our place in it. The dialectical materialist would agree with Dr. Coffin against supinely declaring that war is inevitable. But at that point their ways part. The one turns towards pious hopes and prayer; the other to concrete knowledge and effective organized action.

It may be objected that these are extreme forms of spiritualism and have nothing to do with philosophical idealism. The answer is that in the first place, idealism in general upholds religious ideas, by giving them philosophical support even if at the expense of curbing some of their more extreme tendencies. In the second place, idealism supports all of these attitudes in two ways. First, it makes ideas, our nature, spirit, rather than concrete events (economic conditions, etc.), the cause of social situations and movements. Secondly, it regards ideas as accomplishing results in and by themselves, apart from material forces. This important aspect of idealism has not yet been sufficiently dealt with. In actual daily life it takes the form of holding that what is right will triumph *because* it is *right*. Force, public or mass pressure, actual struggle, are not only unnecessary but interfere with the working of ideas in their purity. It is quite in harmony with idealism for an idealist philosopher to say, as has actually been the case, that he would not support either side in the Spanish rebellion as he couldn't tell which was the right side, but that which ever side was right must necessarily win eventually.

Such is the position of the majority of social reformers. Woodrow Wilson was a tragic exhibition of the failure of this approach. Laying aside the question of his integrity, the fact remains that he helped to bring about great evils after the World War because he pitted *abstract* ideas against the actual forces operating in European diplomacy. Conservative trade union leaders take this position and hope to accomplish great reforms against intrenched power without the attempt to organize a greater actual power behind their ideals than is organized behind their opponents. This attitude goes from the position of opposition to all mass action, all attempts to accomplish desired purposes by material power, to the extreme of creating utopias and then believing that the ideal state imagined will somehow of its own self become transformed into an actual state. And when this does not seem possible the idealist takes refuge, as did Plato after he had presented his outline of an ideal Republic, in saying: "Well ... perhaps in heaven is laid up a pattern of it for him who wishes to behold it ... the question of its present or future existence on earth is quite unimportant."

In sharpest contrast to these attitudes which become organized into a systematic view of the world in the philosophy of idealism, stands the position of materialism. And just as idealism as a philosophy must not be confused with having "ideals," so must philosophical materialism not be confused with materialism in the popular sense of the quest for purely material goods. It is worthy of note that this present age in America is constantly referred to by spiritualists as "materialistic," when actually the dominant philosophy is idealism. It is amusing to notice, conversely, that these same people say that socialism as practiced in the Soviet Union is made into a religion even though dialectical materialism is the accepted philosophy of the U.S.S.R.

Materialism, like idealism, is a systematic world-view that organizes and codifies concrete ways of dealing with problems in man's daily life. It means first of all that every possible occurrence both with regard to man and the world around him is explained by other occurrences or events in our world, and these by others, and so on as far as our knowledge can extend. This is the most fundamental doctrine of all materialism from the Greek philosopher Democritus to the present day. It rules out any and every attempt to understand and explain events by referring them to a supposed power outside of and beyond the world of nature. This is materialism's answer to spiritualism, which consists essentially, as we have seen, in referring events to a power outside of nature. But how do we know, it is asked, that *all* the events of our world can be explained in this manner? The materialist's answer to this question is so important and so fundamental to his whole approach that it requires special consideration.

Before proceeding, however, the reader should be

warned to keep in mind throughout this book that it is not a history of philosophy and that when "the materialist" or "the idealist" is referred to, or the "materialist" position, and so on, it is not meant to imply that all who are or have been called materialists or idealists held the views referred to or were conscious of holding them. Philosophy has had a history of twenty-five hundred years, not to mention the ages preceding when man was making progress in the mastery of nature and in the consciousness of himself. During this historical development of human thought, men often made advances they themselves were not fully aware of, and tended in directions the full meaning of which they could not possibly have understood. Likewise, the social environment in which individual philosophers have lived is extremely complicated and made up of conflicting elements, as was their position in this environment, and thus we should not expect them to have perfectly clear and unequivocal positions. Thus any individual philosopher may have materialist features in his thought in combination with idealist features, as has been, in fact, most often the case. The important point, however, and that on which this treatment rests, is that although there were these confusions and contradictions, the history of philosophical thought becomes meaningful and useful only when we approach it in terms of this fundamental opposition between materialism and idealism.

The basic materialist methodological principle referred to above was probably first advanced by Aristotle. He criticized one of his predecessors, in favor of another, because the second could explain the world as well as the first with only a few principles or assumptions as opposed to an innumerable set of them. He thus introduced a very important idea into philosophy, the idea, namely, that we should not assume any more than we have to. A philosopher in the Middle Ages, William of Occam, formulated this idea systematically, setting forth the important principle that is called "Occam's razor" or the Law of Parsimony. The point of Occam's principle is that it is neither desirable nor legitimate to assume that something exists or causes anything if we can get along without such an assumption. For example, why should we assume that a God caused a birth or a death, a discovery or an earthquake, if we can explain these things just as well by things we actually know to exist? Or, again, why should we explain a man's appearing on earth and teaching certain religious ideas as resulting from an unknown power that controls this world, if we can satisfactorily explain his appearance and teaching by reference to the actual way in which men are born and by which they come to have ideas? Basing himself on this principle, the materialist says, therefore, why should we assume that a God or spiritual force created the universe when we can explain everything that happens without such an assumption? And generalizing still further he argues that one never needs to prove that something does not exist but that *something does exist*. In other words, it is the one who asserts that anything is, who has to prove his assertion. There is no need to trouble about disproving it unless positive evidence can be offered in its favor. Basing himself on this principle, and without this principle there can be no science at all, the materialist contends that he has no need of disproving that there is a God directing the events of this world, and conversely, no right from a scientific point of view to refer anything that happens to a supernatural power. A classic expression of this position was given by the French mathematician and astronomer Laplace who developed in systematic form a theory of the evolution of the solar system. When it was called to his attention that he made no mention of God in his work he replied, "I had no need of that hypothesis."

The second fundamental principle of materialism is really an application of this first insistence that everything be explained "naturally" or by reference to other things we know to exist, to the contention of idealism that the primary reality is mind or spirit. What is this "mind"? the materialist asks. All he knows is processes or events in the world, some of which are called "mental" to distinguish them from those that do not involve consciousness or thinking, feeling, willing, choosing, and the like. "But," the idealist contends, "you regard Mind as an abstraction, as but a name for thinking, feeling, etc. What about your Matter? Is it not equally an abstraction, a name for an unknown substance supposed to lie behind all phenomena?" Many earlier materialists fell into this trap and did not know how to escape it. Modern materialists, however, agree that "matter" is not an abstract something in itself, something behind phenomena, but is a name for all the kinds of things that compose the world, or better still, for all the infinite variety of things and processes our knowledge and our activity reveal. To call them material is to affirm that they are "real" events in space and time, that is, they exist in and of themselves and are not dependent on anything else, whether a God or a mind, for their existence.

Now we are in position to ask what materialism means in practice just as we tried to see what idealism means. It does not mean that only material goods are of value, that life is nothing but food and drink, or that money is the sole good. This is what confused spiritualists may think materialism means and it has been used for more than two thousand years in the attempt to discredit all tendencies away from spiritualism. It does not mean either that there is no such thing as thinking or consciousness. Positively, materialism means, besides the explaining of all events by other events as described above, that thinking and feeling are functions of organized material beings. This involves three important principles.

The materialist, unlike the idealist, does not try to deduce or derive these principles from other beliefs until he comes to something either unknowable or known directly and hence not requiring proof. He shows that they are assumed by us every time we act in practical life and in scientific work, and how all advancing knowledge in the various sciences supports them. Some weak-kneed philosophers, who can't be quite so bold as to be thorough materialists, choose to call them hypotheses. But what meaning is there in calling "hypothetical" (uncertain, merely assumed, not yet established, etc.) those things we know so well that we know them in knowing anything, and which all knowledge in turn makes us understand more fully? The real meaning of doing this is to seem to make materialism a "faith"—something chosen to be believed in just like religion, so that it becomes a mere matter of personal preference what philosophy one has.

The first of these principles is that thinking and feeling have a history. Man, and before him the lower animals, came into a world they did not make. As far as we can tell there were suns and stars and planets before there were any thinking creatures, any "minds." The earth indeed existed for countless ages before there were living organisms upon it, before, consequently, there was thought or feeling. This is what the materialist means when he says that matter is prior to mind: before there were living organisms there was non-living nature, physical processes which had not yet acquired that great degree of complexity and development enabling more complicated forms of behavior than those dealt with in such sciences as physics and chemistry. In maintaining this belief the materialist is clearly not spinning something out of his head but is basing himself on all the best contemporary scientific information we have.

Secondly, thinking and feeling (by these terms we mean to express all the processes of conscious life—

remembering, imagining, perceiving, wishing, choosing, loving, hating, etc.) have a material basis and never appear apart from material organisms. Everywhere we find life processes we find material bodies of definite kinds, and everywhere we find thinking beings we find bodies with a specially organized nervous system, brain, sense organs, and so forth. As bodies their behavior is like that of any other bodies of similar shape and size. They fall to the earth without support according to the same rules by which other bodies fall, and like all physical bodies they did not always exist and will not always exist. But besides behaving according to the general laws of physical motion, they respond to features of their environment in highly specialized and distinctive ways. They have the character, unknown in inanimate nature, of learning, that is, of improving their responses to stimuli around them so that they can adjust themselves ever better to their environment. These special modes of reacting to situations, from mere irritability in lower forms to thought and feeling in men, are however clearly based on the physical organization of these bodies. Injure their brains or nervous apparatus and they can no longer respond in the same ways, and any extensive injury brings loss of the senses, loss of memory, and death. Thus in this respect when the materialist says that matter is prior to mind he means that thinking is a complicated way certain material bodies have of behaving.

The third principle of materialism respecting the relation of matter and mind is more involved and has been less well understood than the other two. It is the belief that all that men think and feel, their characters, personalities, thoughts, choices, desires, loves and hates, arise out of their relation to the world of nature and society. This view, which has been expressed in the phrase "existence determines consciousness," is the direct opposite of the idealist view that consciousness determines existence. It means that ideas do not float down from heaven but arise in men's minds as a result of their contact with the world around them. Some of our ideas are so abstract, so far removed from the things from which they were derived that it has seemed to philosophers that they could not have come from experience at all. This is especially true of numbers and all mathematical ideas. But if we actually study closely the early history of man or even our own children, we find that they gradually come to grasp these abstract ideas from their dealing with, their manipulation of, very concrete things—reindeer or arrows, dolls or balls, and so on. The sciences of anthropology and psychology especially show how men's ideas are obtained in the course of their experience with the world, as opposed to the idealist's efforts to make it appear that the world comes from man's ideas, and hence is dependent on his mind.

But it was not enough for materialists to show that men derived their ideas from the world of nature. The French materialists stopped there, and because of that they failed to explain how men came by more complicated notions such as religious ideas, social conceptions like those of liberty and fraternity, or the notion of human progress. Not being able to refer these ideas to the material world as they understood it, they treated them in either one of two ways. If they liked the ideas, as they did those of liberty, fraternity, and progress, they regarded them as implanted in men by nature from the beginning of time. And if they didn't like them, as they didn't like the idea of man's punishment for Adam's sin, or the idea that a king rules by divine right, they tried to show that these ideas were not *natural* but were foisted upon men by designing and clever priests and aristocrats in order that they might be kept under control and be plundered more easily.

It was Karl Marx and Frederick Engels, the founders of scientific socialism, who first extended the conception of materialism so that this shortcoming was remedied. They showed that the material world meant not only the world of inanimate nature but the world of men as well, and the world of men meant human society or the actual social relations of men. Hence when materialism affirms that existence determines consciousness it must understand that social existence determines social consciousness. In other words, Marx and Engels showed that just as the physical conceptions of men do not simply reflect nature, but are conditioned by the social existence of men, so men's ideas of social questions, of good and evil, liberty and justice, are determined by the social world in which men live and by the individual's position in that social world. This implied that the French philosophers who glorified liberty and fraternity as ideas implanted in man by nature were reading back into the world of nature things that their social position in French society during their time caused them to regard as desirable, just as the ideas that were not to their social interests they thought were faked by misleaders of men. This idea of Marx and Engels means that in the study of history, in the study of all the arts and the sciences and in all the experiences of daily life, we must understand that every idea, every principle, thought or theory, has its own particular history. It once didn't exist; under certain social and historical conditions, it came to be developed by thinking men; it served some function in human life by fulfilling some need (the need may be purely practical or highly theoretical—that is, certain facts require a theory to explain them, or certain theories require some additional theory); and when it no longer fills any need it disappears just as primitive medicine men disappeared when scientific medicine developed. It is very interesting to note that Marx and Engels first gave the world in this doctrine a theory of the history and evolution of human thought that corresponds in its general approach to Darwin's theory of the evolution of animal species, and these two important developments of thought were occurring at the very same time, although Marx and Engels published theirs some years earlier than Darwin.

But we have as yet only sketched the rudiments of this fertile idea. In its more developed form it holds that the economic organization of society, or the way in which men are related one to another in the production of the goods necessary for life, is at the bottom of the political organization of men, their religions, sciences, arts, and philosophies. This aspect of Marxian materialism is commonly referred to as historical materialism, and will be treated in the last chapter along with other conceptions of history. The important thing now is to grasp the dialectical materialist position that all ideas are products of man's interaction with nature and his complex inter-relationships with other men, and that therefore ideas are to be explained by man's material conditions of life, rather than that his conditions of life and the world in general are to be accounted for on the basis of ideas.

We are now in position to sum up the philosophy of materialism and to see it in contrast with idealism. It denies that any God or Gods exist, created, or control the universe. It affirms that there is no reason to believe that something—matter in some form—did not always exist and will not always exist. It denies that the universe had any purpose or is aiming at the accomplishment of anything; only living organisms have purposes, and of these, men alone, as far as we can now tell, are conscious of their purposes and seek to control themselves and the world around them to attain their desires. It affirms that we are a product of this world, were developed in it and by it, and that life on the earth is as natural (that is, is as necessary a result of the nature of things) as the movements of the heavenly bodies, the ebb and flow of the tides, or the sequence of the seasons. It affirms further that man's life within this framework provided by nature is man's own concern and can and will be only what collective man makes it. And finally, materialism insists that all of man's thoughts, feelings, ideals and aspirations, arise out of his position as an organism among other organisms on this particular planet the earth, and out of his particular economic and social development at any given time.

This, however, is only a part of the picture that materialism presents to us. It has to do solely with the nature of the universe in which we live and of ourselves as creatures of such a universe. Another aspect of materialism is its conception of our knowledge and the test of its truth. Materialism affirms that there is no other way of getting knowledge of ourselves and the world than by the methods of the sciences. It denies that there is any so-called higher source of knowledge—a super-worldly experience, divine revelation, intuition, or whatever it may be called. Materialism denies that there is any other source of our ideas than our senses in conjunction with the work of our socially conditioned thinking in interpreting, ordering, and arranging the materials our senses provide us with. It affirms that through our ideas, derived in this way, we can know the world of which we are a part and can test our knowledge by actually trying it out and proving it in experience. It denies that our ideas are the standard by which we judge the nature of things, asserting rather that the nature of things is the sole standard of the truth or falsity of our ideas. It affirms, further, that the needs and desires of men can have no meaning or significance except as men believe them good and desirable in this life here and now.

Putting these two aspects of materialism together, we find it a standard and a basis for our action in the situations that confront us. It means approaching every problem that arises by asking certain kinds of questions, and seeking the answers to them in certain ways. Why did this happen? This means what set or combination of circumstances brought it about, whether it is an eclipse of the sun, an earthquake, technological unemployment, war, or an economic crisis. It means that this question is to be answered scientifically, which is just another way of saying by an actual investigation of the factors, forces, elements, involved, through the use of certain techniques and methods that have been developed in the course of human history and which have been proven successful by the obtaining of workable results, the making of successful predictions, and the opening up of still further knowledge.

Similar methods must be used in determining what is good. This means fulfilling what needs and desires, fulfilling them for whom, what individual, group, or class. This question, too, it can be seen at once, must be answered by the methods just described. War, fascism, imperialism, company unions, collective bargaining, socialism, world peace, prosperity, are all things that some men have called good. How then can we judge? Materialism answers: only by inquiring by scientific methods into the question: who maintains them as good? why? for what purpose? are they what they are claimed to be? what will be their results in practice? etc. All this is in sharpest contrast to idealism, which is a much easier way to follow. It never needs to ask such difficult questions and engage in the strenuous effort of answering them. It can say always in answer to the questions concerning how and why something happens and what is good: it happened because God willed it, it is good because God decreed it, it must have been designed to serve some good purpose, or it is good because it will make us happy in a future life. This path is easier but it can be disastrous. It requires less effort only at the expense of placing us at the mercy of the forces of nature and the forces of the men who happen at any time to be in a dominant position in relation to their fellows.

But Marxian materialism means more than asking questions and answering them. As a philosophy, it insists on the connection, the unity, of theory and practice, on pointing out that the solving of problems requires more than thinking correctly about them. It means changing conditions by means of our knowledge in accordance with our requirements, when these have been examined in the light of what is possible of attainment. In this way, through men's understanding it, the philosophy of materialism becomes an actual force in the world, as strong a force for accomplishing human purposes as idealism is a force for circumventing them. But to remain materialistic, we must see that materialism is not a force in virtue of its being an idea, but only in virtue of its being a weapon in actual social life. Materialism carried into practice has thus the same sense as radicalism. Radicalism literally means getting at the roots of a thing. Materialism means getting at the matter or to the bottom of it, finding its basis and its causes. This is in fact what materialism meant to the rising middle class seeking power in eighteenth-century France, and has meant since Marx and Engels to the nineteenth- and twentieth-century working class.

Dialectical materialism is therefore in all its aspects an organized theory and a way of life directly opposite to that of idealism. It is a way both of understanding the world and of changing it. As the first it embraces the theory and practice of science. As the second, it is a weapon for social progress when translated into appropriate action on the part of those classes of men whose needs and interests impel them towards a new social order. Over the gateway to the great old monastery of Kiev, in the U.S.S.R., is now inscribed a motto which is a striking application of materialism to the problems of the oppressed and downtrodden of the old Czarist Empire: "Do not think that any God or Gods can save you. Only the united efforts of workers and farmers can remove the yoke of oppression."

III. PERMANENCE
AND CHANGE

CAN HUMAN NATURE CHANGE? — SOCIAL BASIS OF A STATIC WORLD-VIEW — PLATO — CHRISTIANITY — NEWTONIAN PHYSICS — RISE OF EVOLUTIONARY BELIEFS — FRENCH AND AMERICAN REVOLUTIONS — ARISTOTELIAN CONCEPTION OF DEVELOPMENT — STATIC LIMITATIONS OF EIGHTEENTH-CENTURY MATERIALISM — HEGELIAN DIALECTICS AS A THEORY OF CHANGE — TRANSFORMATION AND APPLICATION OF DIALECTICS BY MARX AND ENGELS — THE DIALECTICAL CONCEPTION OF THE WORLD

"YOU can't change human nature." This statement, used daily as a conclusion to a political argument, reveals not only a person's politics, but his philosophy as well. It is just another way of saying, "Human nature is human nature," and belongs in a great general class of statements known technically as tautologies. "Whatever is, is"; "Women are women"; "Boys will be boys"; and best of all, "Business is business," are all expressions of profound conviction which preclude further discussion. They reveal an attitude of mind, a conception of society, and a whole theory of the universe. This is none the less a philosophy for want of a name. It cuts across both materialism and idealism, and like both of these, has its own particular opposite. In short, it is not enough to know whether a type of thinking is materialistic or idealistic, but also whether it regards things as fixed and limited once and for all, or conceives of everything as in a process of change.

The belief that you can't change human nature clearly presupposes that there is something fixed and given that can be called the nature of man, that he was made that way in the beginning and will remain so till the end. It means further that nothing can change or affect what man is, but what he *is* will determine all that he does and ever can do. Those who assert this generally mean much more than that man doesn't change. They assume that the world doesn't change, that society doesn't change, that the economic order cannot and does not change. All the evidence we have, however, shows that the world is constantly changing, that animal species change, society and economic forms and men have always been undergoing changes, now slowly and now more rapidly, but changing nevertheless. Perhaps those who maintain this view do not pretend to base their position on facts or evidence. They seem to assert, rather, that something is as it is and they intend to try to keep it that way. "Business is business" means that business practices may not be very ethical and may require hard dealing, but nothing can or should be done about it. He who says, "There have always been wars and there always will be," takes the same position. The ordinary man who employs this manner of thought little dreams that for more than two thousand years philosophers have developed elaborate methods to prove just this same thing—that what is real does not change, and conversely, that what changes is not real. Change is reduced to the status of mere *appearance,* illusory being, while reality is held to be eternally fixed and changeless.

It is not hard to see that since philosophers, as men of sufficient economic means to have the leisure to spend their lives in thinking, have almost always been members of the dominant economic class in society, they have reflected the views of their class. Further, it is clear that for those in superior economic position change is likely to appear always as change for the worse, and thus while they try to prevent change in practice, they abolish it *in theory.* Thus have developed systematic ways of denying change, motion, process, and of glorifying the fixed and immobile.

The worlds of Plato and Aristotle, of Descartes and Spinoza, to name two of the greatest ancient and two of the greatest modern philosophers, all illustrate this attitude towards time and change. Plato developed an elaborate theory of a changeless reality. The real consisted of the forms, species or types of things, while the actual things of our world were only relatively illusory appearances or temporary embodiments of these eternal entities. This was perhaps due to certain attitudes of thought that were developing among Greek philosophers (we have already seen that the earliest Greek thinkers had evolutionary conceptions of the world) and to Plato's social position in the Athenian society of his day. He not only expressed his static conceptions of the world in his philosophy but also in his aesthetic and political judgments. He praised Egyptian art above

Greek art because he thought its forms never changed, and his ideal Republic was a state conceived as absolutely "frozen." To Plato its very quality of being "ideal" implied that it couldn't possibly be subject to any manner of change. Aristotle paid some homage to change and development, as we shall see, but he carefully circumscribed it and remained too close to Plato and the traditional conceptions of his day to give up a changeless pattern of the world.

The rise of Christianity and its dominance over Western thought for the past two thousand years further developed and solidified a static view of the world. According to the Christian tradition God made the world and all that is in it all at once (or in a few days) not so many thousands of years ago. Just what happened before this relatively recent date is not very clear, but there are rumors of angels revolting and of other heavenly disorders. The world having thus been made, its limits defined, and all the species of animals created each according to a particular pattern, the only things that happen have more to do with the heavenly drama of salvation than with earthly change. God could not change, it is held, because he would have to change either for the better or for the worse. He could not change for the better because he is perfect, and likewise, being perfect, he could not change for the worse. Once God is thus conceived, it easily follows that the world, being his handiwork, is likewise not subject to any real change, for its change would seem to imply that God did not make it properly in the first place.

During the vast social and intellectual movements of the European Renaissance, change came to be recognized and relatively dynamic conceptions of the world were developed, but this soon gave way once more to static views. These were reinforced by the development of Newtonian physics. Sir Isaac Newton, having discovered and set forth certain fundamental laws of motion, especially the law of gravitation concerning the attraction of every body in space to every other body, thought that he had thus brought to light the very laws in accordance with which God had designed the universe. He conceived of God as having created the physical world just as it now exists and as having imposed laws upon it, as can be seen from the following passage from his famous work, *Mathematical Principles:* "This most beautiful system of the sun, planets, and comets, could only proceed from the counsel and dominion of an intelligent and powerful Being. And if the fixed stars are the centers of other like systems, these, being formed by the like wise counsel, must be all subject to the dominion of One; especially since the light of the fixed stars is of the same nature with the light of the sun, and from every system light passes into all the other systems: and lest the systems of the fixed stars should, by their gravity, fall on each other, he hath placed those systems at immense distances from one another." The principles and method of the Newtonian physics thus caused men to ignore the whole problem of change. Motion or change exists only within a rigid and changeless framework and although the world might seem to present a scene of constant motion it is a motion that never goes anywhere.

It was not until the period just preceding and during the French Revolution that a changing or dynamic view of the world began to come into its own. It seemed to appear first in the belief that man was capable of unlimited social progress. There was no limit to man's inherent capability of development. Only bad social institutions held him back. It is important to note that it was during this same period, the latter part of the eighteenth century, that Lamarck was developing a theory of animal evolution and Kant and Laplace the theory of the evolution of the whole solar system itself.

This was the beginning of one of the greatest revolutions in the whole history of thought. It was contemporary with the rise of what is known as romanticism. All limits, bounds, fixed forms are to be broken down, and an untold wealth of possibilities are conceived as lying before us. The men who held these revolutionary views tended towards materialism, while their opponents were on the whole spiritualists. But materialism, as it had been developed up to this time, was not able fully and adequately to digest and interpret the new emphasis on change and process. Part of this is due to social factors. The leaders of the French Revolution had to use as allies the workers of the cities and the peasantry. But once the immediate aim of the revolution was accomplished, they had to turn against the "excesses," as they called them, of their allies, compromise with their former enemies, and set up a system of society that fell short of fulfilling the interests of all classes in society. This received its philosophical expression in putting the brakes on the idea of ceaseless change. Similarly in America James Madison, John Adams, and Alexander Hamilton, for example, who were leaders of the classes that came into power by the American Revolution, held to ideas of human nature as not changing, of there being a natural distinction between "the rich and well-born and the rest of the people" and of establishing a "government destined to remain forever."

It is most interesting that the Americans named here were all spiritualists, while the men who wanted to carry the revolution further in America, men like Elihu Palmer, Benjamin Rush, Thomas Cooper, and John Taylor, all tended more towards the materialist side. Jefferson remained in between, but was sufficiently on the side of materialism to be denounced publicly by the conservatives as a materialist and an atheist. Alexander Hamilton blamed materialism for the excesses of the French Revolution, and denounced all Americans who sought the practical fulfillment of the principles of the Declaration of Independence as questioning the "very existence of a Deity," and as asserting "the perishable nature of man,"—in short, of being materialists.

But there were fundamental theoretical difficulties as well, in the way of adequate recognition of a changing world, in eighteenth-century philosophy.

The French philosophers, such as LaMettrie, Helvetius, Diderot, and Holbach, however materialistic they may have wanted to be, were subject to certain limitations because of the development of thought up to their day. One of these limitations was the lack of an historical approach to problems and institutions. While on the one hand eighteenth-century French philosophers were beginning to recognize the possibility of ceaseless change, they failed to see the present as an actual product of the past. They failed to trace the actual course of the development of human institutions and ideas, including their own. This made it difficult if not impossible for them to view their activity in the light of its historical background and future direction. One instance of this has already been seen in their use of such terms as Liberty and Equality. But it goes deeper, extending to their conceptions of institutions like the monarchy, the union of church and state, feudal economic relations, as well as to the nature of the institutions and relations they would substitute for these. They thought, for example, that by bringing the doctrines of the Christian church to the light of reason they would destroy these doctrines and the organized church. This followed from their naïve conception that religion was just something foisted upon gullible men by scheming deceivers. Had they actually studied the church and its teachings historically, they would have understood it better and learned that religion was an expression of human needs and aspirations which would remain as long as these particular needs and aspirations could not be satisfied in any more real and genuine way in actual life. Likewise, not understanding the historical development of feudalism, its rise, and its decline in the face of new and powerful forces requiring unrestricted trade, free-dom of investment, a free labor market, etc., they thought that these new interests they represented were the interests of all men rather than of a very limited number who would profit at the expense of the masses of their fellows. Another example of their static mode of thought when dealing with concrete questions was their use of the doctrine of "natural rights." This doctrine that certain rights belong to men by nature and therefore cannot be taken away by any government made a valuable revolutionary slogan, but the static conceptions involved in it allowed its conversion in the nineteenth century into "vested" or property rights and hence into a static principle of the capitalist order. In general we can say that although the eighteenth-century philosophers were beginning to think of things as changing they had not yet learned to apply this view toward the understanding of the existing social institutions.

Another serious limitation was the inability to explain man's activity in making and remaking institutions, in creating and re-creating his external environment, including the physical and social worlds. While they were materialists and sought to explain men by reference to their environment, they failed to grasp the fact that men react on their environment and in so doing create new conditions which in turn change men. This arose from the failure to apply fully the idea of all things as changing and as acting upon one another in the process. Part of this shortcoming was due to a general lack of theoretical development, which will be shown later, and part to the fact that these men had nothing better to base themselves on than the theories of John Locke, philosopher of the English revolution a century earlier. Locke sought vigorously to establish that our ideas come only from experience, but he had a completely artificial conception of the nature of man's experience. Instead of it consisting of our actual activity in a world of social beings, to Locke it was something that took place in the individual's head. He thought of the individual as a purely passive device for recording the ideas knocked into his mind by things outside, and he distrusted any ideas that might appear to have been made by man himself. Knowledge was thus not something represented by the sciences and the practical activity of men, but a mere copy in each individual's head of the things outside. This theory of knowledge enabled men to show easily enough that we are products of our environment, but it did not enable them to show how by knowing this environment and how it acts upon us, we can change it as our needs and desires require. They might have been able to explain how wretched living conditions produce crime and drunkenness, and how these in turn create worse conditions which become breeding grounds for further crime, and how this makes life more wretched still. But they could not quite explain the fact that by knowing this vicious circle we can act on our knowledge and thus make new conditions which will change men. It is partly for such theories as these that the eighteenth-century philosophers are called "mechanical." It is because a machine is the model to them of all process and movement. Men are at the mercy of the environment as the wheel of an engine is at the mercy of the driving shaft. It was only in Germany in the nineteenth century that a full solution was provided for this difficulty.

It has been seen that there are two fundamentally opposed philosophies: materialism and idealism. Cutting across these we have found a further conflict of positions: the one viewing the world as fixed and static, disparaging change as unreal and illusory, the other conceiving everything as in motion. We have now indicated some of the ways in which the second view came to triumph over the first and have seen that even when change was recognized as a fundamental aspect of things some of the old ideas still prevented a complete revolution in our thinking. It is clearly not enough merely to recognize change as universal and all-pervasive. A further question is involved. How do process, motion, evolution and development come about? The suggestion has already been made that universal motion and development are minimized if they are regarded as taking place only within fixed and rigid limits. There are two aspects of this question which will have to be dealt with separately. The first has to do with the theory of evolution developed by Aristotle, the second with the method of dealing with motion employed in the early history of modern physical science.

Aristotle sought some method of understanding and interpreting the changes which we see taking place in the world, for example, the growth of an animal from the beginning of the embryo to maturity, or the development of the acorn into an oak. Modern students interpret Aristotle as dealing only with the question of the growth of individuals. Perhaps Aristotle himself was not clear as to just what he was doing. He took over many of the ideas of Plato, which ideas would make the evolution of species impossible or would at least make it unimportant or meaningless. On the other hand there were opposing tendencies in his thought. The question is to us relatively unimportant. The fact remains that many modern idealists use Aristotle's principles to interpret biological evolution (that is, the evolution of species) in order to *minimize* or *play down* such evolution.

Aristotle insisted that the basis of all thought, and consequently of all reality, is the principle of contradiction—that a thing cannot at the same time both have a property and not have that property. Thus, whatever properties of things we might take: redness, hardness, intelligence, two-leggedness, etc., any given thing either has such properties or does not have them. Yet at the same time he sought to do justice to the obvious fact that things change. He concluded therefore that a thing can become only what it potentially is, and that whatever a thing does become is its reality or actuality. Now in plain English this means nothing more nor less than saying that nothing becomes anything that it did not have the *possibility* of becoming, or that what anything actually and fully is was always really *there,* in it, from the beginning. This was a clever theory and an important contribution to man's thought. It recognized change and saw that there is continuity in change, or that for any *thing* to be thought of as changing, *it* had to retain its identity throughout the process. But it failed to recognize the other aspect of change, namely, its discontinuity. It could explain change only up to the present, only within carefully defined limits, only when both the beginning and the supposed end were already known. And nothing ever *really* happens, for whatever becomes of a thing was already there from the very beginning. It was essentially a conservative theory which, while paying lip service to change, makes the change only in the past and tends to regard things as we now know them, as the real and actual things and therefore not subject to change in the future.

Perhaps this can be better understood if applied to a present-day problem of interest to all men. The fact that the capitalist mode of production involves the socialization of the actual process of production, that is, that many men come together and labor socially to produce a single type of product, watches, automobiles, structural steel, has made some men think that socialism is already rooted in capitalist society. Therefore, using Aristotle's ideas, they argue that socialism is potentially contained in capitalism, or that capitalism is potential socialism. The inevitable conclusion is that socialism will therefore gradually emerge from capitalism, or, in other words, that capitalism will of itself flower into socialism. It is interesting to notice that when eighteenth-century materialists used this same mode of approach in explaining life they reached similar conclusions. Since life appears in a material world, or out of matter, it must have been in matter in the first place, and thus they tried to picture every atom or particle of matter as having the potentiality or possibility of life within it. This did not really *explain* anything but only gave the appearance of explanation by pushing the problem back one step farther. It should be clear from these examples that Aristotle's conception, valuable as it may have been in the history of thought, did not allow for a satisfactory conception of the world as constantly developing *new* forms, as giving rise to new relations and therefore to new laws.

The second of the approaches to motion and change that tended to keep them confined to fixed limits was closely tied up with the new scientific developments that culminated in the seventeenth century. New methods of studying nature came to be employed during this period and tremendous discoveries were made. Out of new needs of men and new social conditions developed the possibility and necessity of ocean navigation, of the mining of minerals on a larger scale, of the production of more effective instruments of warfare, etc. Through these needs the sciences of physics, mechanics, chemistry, and astronomy, were developed to new and higher stages. The most important of these advances came about through the use of the experimental method and the development of new techniques for the application of mathematics to the physical world. Now the fact that such physical phenomena as the falling of a body to the earth, the movement of the earth about the sun, or the relation of the volume of a gas to the pressure under which it is kept, could be expressed in simple mathematical equations, led the great scientists of the age (such men as Galileo, Descartes, Boyle, and Newton) to believe that over, above, and apart from the material world was a realm of rational relations. Or, to put it more simply, that before there was any change there were the unchanging principles or laws of change and motion and hence that all change took place only within an unchanging framework. As is to be expected, God was held to be the creator of the eternal laws to which the physical world must conform. This is a very human conception of *law,* for it converts the discovered uniformities in nature into fixed principles imposed upon nature and which material things *must* obey. This attitude may have arisen in part from the fact that it enabled these scientists to pursue their new course of investigations and still keep peace with Christian traditions. It may also have been encouraged and reinforced by the need these men were under to show that they were not reading their own ideas into nature but were discovering the very principles which governed nature.

Whatever the causes of this position, there were two bad effects of it. First, it led these scientists and their followers to believe that whatever had happened in the past and would happen in the future comes about not in virtue of the things themselves in their inter-relationships, but because of the eternal laws of the universe under which they operate. This conception, just like Plato's, makes the world static and change unimportant. Secondly, the conception of a fixed system of laws in conjunction with the successes of this new science in the realm of physics gave rise to the view that all the phenomena of nature (the human soul excepted, since it was considered not to be a part of this physical world) were purely mechanical and were to be conceived solely in terms of the motion in space, collision, and rebounding, etc., of so many particles of matter. This led to what has been known as reductivism, or the theory that mechanics, as the science of the motion of particles of matter, was the basic and model science and the one to which all other knowledge should be reduced.

Men who followed this view, of whom Holbach of eighteenth-century France can be taken as an example, admitted that we were far from this goal, but tended to regard the existence of any other sciences such as biology or politics as due to our ignorance. Unfortunately, too, this came to be regarded as the *materialist* way of looking at things. These men, in their opposition to the church and the spiritualist viewpoint, sought to find the causes of everything in matter, but did not see that the material world is not just matter in the abstract but material things organized in more or less complicated ways and behaving in accordance with more or less complicated principles. In the eighteenth century this was still a progressive standpoint, for it gave the French thinkers a position from which they could attack superstition and insist on the importance of the material conditions of man's life. But since that time it has become more and more reactionary, and today it comes dangerously close to spiritualism, as in the impossibility of explaining the complexities of our world in simple mechanical terms, it tends to support the hypothesis of an unknown and unknowable something behind the events of our biological and social world. Herbert Spencer well represents the beginning of this tendency. He started out by talking about an "unknown" behind appearances. Soon this was converted into an "unknowable" and finally it became *the* Unknowable, or just another name for God. In spite of all of Spencer's talk about evolution, his world was static nevertheless. Behind it was the great Unknowable and all evolution took place in accordance with a fixed law which he thought he had discovered and which was imposed upon matter, perhaps by the Unknowable.

Again it is to German philosophy of the last century that we must turn for a solution of these difficulties and for a systematically developed conception of all things as undergoing ceaseless change. And it was the philosopher Hegel who first gave the best account of a completely evolving universe. Even to this day Hegel is opposed by those thinkers who like to put all things into neat compartments and to think of the universe as a fixed and changeless system. Hegel's was the first great philosophical system to break down the traditional philosophical view of a completed and fixed universe that dominated most Western thought from Plato to Spinoza. Like other great originators in the history of thought, Hegel was not fully conscious of what he had done and did it only incompletely. But the good Christians of Germany in his time came more and more to fear what Hegel had done, and not long after his death all "Hegelians" were removed from positions in the University of Berlin. And as Karl Marx remarked, this philosophy of change shocked the ruling classes of the time, for they could not lightly face a philosophy which implied that they were only temporarily the ruling class, and that just as other forms of society had gone before them others still would come after. Hegel himself tried to tone down this aspect of his philosophy and tried to make it appear that the existing Prussian state was the final and highest form of human political development.

In spite of all of Hegel's shortcomings, which are rooted in the idealist nature of his philosophy, he accomplished one great important task. He cut through, with one stroke, the whole traditional idea of the universe as a static, permanent, timeless system of things, and conceived everything as in motion, as in process of change. This new view supersedes both the Aristotelian conception of change and the mechanism of the seventeenth- and eighteenth-century philosophers and scientists.

In this account of Hegel it is not to be assumed that Hegel thought of all these things in just this way. His system of philosophy is confused by conflicting notions and attitudes. On one side is the dialectical method, and on the other the Absolute in the form of eternal Reason existing in and through all things. What is of importance to us here is what Hegel has meant to the progressive thinkers since his time, who have learned to use what is progressive in him. Just one example: Hegel's conception of things as in flux implies that time is a central concept in philosophy (which it was not for Plato, Spinoza and others) but yet Hegel strangely contrives to keep time out of the picture in his greatest single work, the *Science of Logic*. Still one of the most important influences of Hegel's thought on all subsequent philosophy has been the recognition of time as a fundamental category of the universe.

Since Hegel, the traditional timeless world of the great classical philosophers is out of date. The world is no longer a limited, changeless, boxed-in universe. Everything is in motion and new things arise with the passing of time, and likewise, as the world evolves, new laws come into being as new and more complicated material structures arise. But all this can best be understood by means of a few examples. We have seen that, following the Aristotelian conception of the evolution of something, socialism is contained as a germ within capitalism and can be expected gradually to emerge from it as an oak emerges from an acorn. Hegel's theory does away with this idea of gradual development. In one striking passage he pictures the form of the new society arising within the womb of the old until it bursts forth from it just as a chicken bursts the shell of the egg in which it was contained. Of course as Hegel saw, the new society does not emerge fullfledged, but must fight its way until it is full grown and the remnants of the old society are destroyed.

If you ask now, will capitalism evolve into socialism, the answer still is yes, but the process is conceived in an entirely different way. Marx, following Hegel, held that capitalism contains the germs of socialism, but as a contradiction within it. The processes of production are socialized in that large numbers of men combine their labor to produce a single type of product. But appropriation remains individualized. The owner or owners of the factory have sole possession and control of this product of socialized labor. This produces a contradiction between the mode of production and the economic organization of the productive process. This contradiction expresses itself in the periodic crises of capitalism, as well as in strikes, the use of the police power of the state to suppress the workers, in war, as well as in revolutionary uprisings. Thus capitalism contains the germs of socialism in itself, and will evolve into socialism, but only through the destruction of itself. The new social form is struggling within the old and will emerge from it not gradually but through an upheaval in which the old disappears and the new takes its place. It is easy to see that this conception of change or evolution, just like the Aristotelian one, preserves the continuity in the process, but it does not do so by ignoring or destroying the discontinuity.

Right here, in this application of Hegel's conception of evolution, known as the dialectical method, to social problems, we see the difference between certain liberals socialistically inclined, such as reformist Socialists or the British Fabians and the Marxists. In this method we see the roots of the doctrine that the inherent contradictions of capitalism will eventually cause its downfall, that the workers are the grave-diggers of capitalism, and that capitalism is a system which breeds the means for its own overthrow. It is truly difficult to imagine the development of this theory without the help that the philosophy of Hegel gave to Karl Marx.

Or let us take another problem, one that caused trouble to the mechanistic thinkers of the eighteenth century. Is mechanics the model science to which all knowledge should be reduced? That view is based on the notion that a thing is nothing but the sum of its parts, and since all things are made up of material particles in motion, their behavior is merely the sum total of the motions of their parts. For Hegel's method, a thing is not merely the sum of its parts. As matter becomes more complicated in its organization, takes on more complex patterns, it acquires new modes of behavior. The new pattern or structure—the oxygen atom, the water molecule, protoplasm, or the brain of man—not only contains all the processes of simpler forms of matter, but has new modes of action, is capable of *new* and more complicated patterns of behavior. Hence new and more complicated laws are necessary to describe this behavior, and we have the independent sciences of chemistry, biology, psychology, and so on. Here Hegel offers a solution to the problem that baffled earlier scientists and which many later ones have not yet learned to solve. Hegel's principle can be stated something like this: as you increase the amount of anything, you sometimes get not only more of the same thing but something new, you have changed its quality as well as its quantity. Or again, as the organization of anything becomes more complicated, it not only reacts to other things or behaves in the same way it did before, but rather at a given point it reacts or behaves in new and different ways. As the brain of the higher apes, for example, became larger, more complex and delicate in its organization, as the species evolved, it performed not only more of the same kind of operations but was able to acquire new functions—as represented in part by the use of language. Life itself can now be better understood than it was by the eighteenth-century French materialists. They tended to take the position that since life arises in a material world, it must have been inherent in matter in the first place, and thus they read life back into the supposed units of matter. Using Hegel's principle, we can see how, as matter became more and more complex in its organization, it was capable of new and more complicated modes of behavior—those forms of behavior to which we give the name life.

Thus in all fields of thought this principle of Hegel's offers us the solution of many baffling problems. It is no longer necessary, because one is a materialist, to seek to reduce all phenomena to the laws of mechanics. Mechanics has to do only with matter in certain elementary forms, as bodies occupying space. But matter not only occupies space and is subject to the universal law of gravity. It also appears in an infinite gradation of forms, more or less complicated, and thus is established the autonomy of the various sciences—physical, biological, and social. Each of these sciences exists in its own right as dealing with matter at different stages or levels of organization.

Modern physics, since the discovery of the electron, has shown that this principle works both ways. Just as mechanics, the science of the motion of bodies in space was not adequate to handle more complex organizations of matter, neither was it capable of handling the more minute elements of matter, the sub-atomic processes. Idealist philosophers immediately raised the cry that "matter" had disappeared and that materialism therefore was rendered impossible. But what really happened was merely that these new discoveries showed that the older classic mechanics was too crude to handle satisfactorily these newly discovered material processes.

We might also take a few examples of Hegel's principle from the social world. An employer discovers that he can cut the wages of his workers five cents an hour and he does so. He then tries it again and is again successful. But he invariably is brought to the point where a new cut so arouses his workers that they organize and strike. Likewise, a strike is primarily a form of economic activity. It is a form of struggle engaged in by workers for the protection and promotion of their economic interests. But let there come a wave of strikes, culminating perhaps in a great general strike. It ceases to be merely economic activity. Political demands are raised, as in France in 1936 before the advent of the People's Front government, and the strike ends with wide political changes as well as economic ones.

Thus in all spheres of nature and of human life, itself a part of nature, we find ceaseless change which is not a mere repetition of the same processes, but in which new things and processes arise. The world is a developing world and human society never remains fixed nor does it revolve in a closed circle. Certain directions are to be found in its development, which will be discussed in chapter five. All this Hegel expressed in the opening chapters of his work on Logic. Traditional philosophy from Plato on had started with some one fixed reality—Being, Substance, God, the Real —and had always conceived it as there once and for all through all eternity. But Hegel rejects the concept of Being on the grounds that mere Being, pure Being (or as we would be more likely to put it, being everything in general and nothing in particular) is indistinguishable from Nothing. Then he shows that the first idea with which he can begin is the idea of Becoming. This idea of Becoming is the combination of the ideas of Being and Nothing but not a mere mixing together of the two. What Hegel seems to mean is that anything that really exists is a particular thing and is not something else and is in constant movement as a result of its own inherent nature and its interactions with other things in the universe.

Hegel used three expressions to represent this dy-

namic character of the universe, this new conception
of the nature of development and change. The first is
called the "unity of opposites." Being and Nothing are
opposites, as opposite as any two things or ideas can
be, and yet together they constitute something, namely,
becoming. The second he called the "negation of negation," by which he meant, to use the example of Being
and Nothing given above, that being is negated by nothing and that nothing is in turn negated by becoming.
In general, Hegel was seeking to show by these principles that something developing, being moved forward by the contradictions within it, does not just
unfold itself but is negated, is destroyed by its opposite
which has been generated within it, and that this in
turn is negated, and through this process something
new emerges. He was thinking primarily of an argument or a thought-process in which a one-sided statement is made that is negated by its own inner
contradictions, leading to the assertion of its opposite
or negation. But this second statement, being merely
the negation of the first, is also one-sided, and gives
rise to a new statement which is the negation of the
second (that is, the negation of the original negation)
and thus is something positively new and not just the
original statement over again.

Marx and Engels saw these principles of dialectics
as the laws of all motion and change, both in nature
and society, but they also saw that they required a
complete transformation from the form they were
given by Hegel. Marx said of this in his great work

Capital that his dialectical method is not only different from the Hegelian but is its direct opposite. "To Hegel," he continues, "the life-process of the human brain, i.e., the process of thinking, which under the name of 'the idea,' he even transforms into an independent subject, is the demiurgos of the real world, and the real world is only the external, phenomenal form of 'the Idea.' With me, on the contrary, the ideal is nothing else than the material world reflected by the human mind, and translated into forms of thought. ... The mystification which dialectic suffers in Hegel's hands, by no means prevents him from being the first to present its general form of working in a comprehensive and conscious manner. With him it is standing on its head. It must be turned right side up if you would discover the rational kernel within the mystical shell." Marx used this materialist dialectic in discovering the "laws of motion" of capitalist society and of the transition to socialism. He saw capitalism as a unity of opposites—the socialized nature of the productive process and the individualized nature of the appropriation of the means and the product of production—which is reflected in the opposition of the working class to the capitalist class which owns the instruments of production. The dictatorship of the proletariat is the negation of the capitalist state, while the attainment of a communist society is the negation of this negation.

Hegel's third expression was that quantity is transformed into quality. This we have already analyzed.

One example Hegel gave was that of a particular political system in a society. Make that society larger and larger, he said, and sooner or later the political organization of that society will have to change; a contradiction will arise between the old form and the new content. He was thinking, perhaps, of the difference in government between the Greek city-state or a Swiss canton, and the Roman Empire or modern states like France or England. Marx used this expression to describe the fact that as the contradictions between labor and capital increased not only was there more of the class struggle but it reached new levels or stages, until a breaking point came and the class struggle emerged in a new form as the dictatorship of the proletariat.

We are now in position to sum up some of the central ideas of the modern dialectical conception of the universe that developed largely through Hegel's influence. This can best be done under the following main heads:

1. Time must be a central concept of all philosophical systems. For the earlier philosophers time was something which could be left out of the reckoning as they considered it irrelevant to the logical structure of the world. Spinoza represented this perfectly in his ideal of knowledge as the seeing of things *"sub specie aeternitatis"* (under the form of•eternity). This meant knowing things solely in terms of their *logical* relations to the whole of the nature and hence as abstracted from all temporal process. But now the flow or movement of things in time is alone real, and things thought

of as not being in time, as not beginning and ending, are but the shadows of things abstracted from their reality. The development of things in time and the study of their changes assumes the place formerly occupied exclusively by what the philosophers thought of as the logical relations of things. This has important consequences for all human life, as can easily be seen when we turn to ideas of what is good, right, beautiful, etc. These were once supposed to be eternal things, having no relation to time and the observed changes in man's social world. Now they are seen as relative to particular conditions and situations and hence as changing with the changing conditions of life.

2. To understand anything we must study it historically, must see how it came to be the thing it is and determine the direction in which it is moving. We might take as an illustration the American Constitution. The conservatives treat it as if it were somehow handed down by God and was hence sacred and inviolable. They claim that it is based on eternal principles of justice and right and therefore conclude that it cannot be improved, while in practice they flout it whenever it is to their interests to do so. But when we learn to approach things historically we study the particular conditions under which the Constitution was written, analyze the social and economic forces in the American states in 1787 and their development from the time of the Declaration of Independence eleven years earlier, and inquire precisely into the purposes and interests the framers had in mind in devising this

instrument of government. Then we analyze it today in the light of the present needs and interests of the American people and learn to what extent it is adequate or inadequate to accomplish its avowed end of promoting the well-being of our people.

Another striking example is found in the difference between the classic bourgeois economists, Adam Smith and Ricardo, and Marx and Engels. For the former, capitalism simply exists as the system it is. They neither thought of it as having a history nor as moving in a specific direction. For them it was a self-equilibrating system whose inner workings could be analyzed without reference to time or history. For Marx and Engels, imbued with Hegelian ideas of process, capitalism was an economic system which arose through certain historical trends and which, through its own inherent dynamics of development, would eventually be superseded by another economic system.

We must learn to see every institution as arising out of particular conditions, as developing in particular ways, and as coming to serve better or worse the purposes for which it was brought into being. It is important to grasp how this view of the universe as in constant process leads necessarily to the study of all customs, traditions, and institutions in their historical development.

3. Finally, this conception of things as processes, of things as evolving and changing their forms requires the substitution of organic terms for atomic and mechanical ones. Things or processes must be seen as

wholes, made up of inter-acting parts, and themselves as functioning within still larger wholes which constitute their environment. For this reason we cannot make an absolute separation of economics from politics and vice versa, but should deal with the two in their inter-relationship as historical materialism teaches. For this reason we cannot talk about democracy or dictatorship in the abstract. There is capitalist democracy and socialist democracy, and there is the dictatorship of the proletariat, and the fascist dictatorship of Germany and Italy. In the same way we cannot talk about knowledge in terms simply of ideas in our minds and nature or external things outside our minds, but must speak of the interaction of nature in man with nature outside of man. Nor can we speak of insanity as merely psychological or physiological, but must think of it in terms of the inability of the *organism as a whole* to meet the problems which the environment puts before it.

We are now in position to draw certain broad conclusions from our examination of these two opposed views of the universe. It should once again be emphasized that they cut across the lines of materialism and idealism. But however true this is, one cannot fail to notice that idealism cannot do justice to the dynamic, changing nature of things. In general the idealists seek to limit this change, for if mind or spirit is the inner nature or essence of things, or that without which nothing can be, then mind or spirit existed from all eternity and has its own nature which does not change. Further, idealists tend to think of the world as having some goal or end set before it, a goal implicit in mind or spirit, and thus those who embrace a dynamic view still confine development within the fixed limits imposed upon it by eternal mind. There is no such limitation, however, upon materialism, and it can freely conceive all things as in change with nothing static or permanent in all the universe. Henri Bergson, a contemporary French philosopher, who had for a period a large popular following, represents those few spiritualists who hold for a completely dynamic universe. But the interesting thing about his thought is that his dynamism, as was the case with Nietzsche, is carried to such extremes that knowledge is conceived as utterly false and misleading since it supposedly embraces things only as fixed. Thus we find an idealism which pretends to do justice to change but only at the cost of claiming to deprive us of all scientific knowledge in the interests of a mystical and mythical *intuition*.

It should be clear by this time that there is a psychological and social difference between these two positions. Those who are well established in society, who prosper or think they prosper by the existing state of things and who fear that they have something to lose by a change, like to feel their position guaranteed by the nature of things, like everything neatly delimited, would feel lost in any world but one in which "East is East and West is West, And never the twain shall meet"—these shun the idea of change and hold dearly to what they conceive as the permanent reality over and above the apparent change of things. Those, on the other hand, who suffer through their inferior economic and social status or who by various causes are led to view society from the standpoint of the under-privileged endlessly seek for new things, have faith in man and the possibility of his unlimited progress, and abhorring the idea of a boxed-in universe feel free only in an infinitely developing world.

But the psychological differences between these two views are less important than the social differences. In fact, of course, the two cannot be separated since each man's psychology or temperament develops only in a social environment and bears some relation to it. Now throughout all historical periods society has witnessed economic and social conflicts centering around the distribution of property and the type of economic relations. Except in primitive communist society, there have always been (until the Russian Revolution) the relatively few who owned property, and who in virtue of that ownership controlled the society, set its moral standards, made its laws, and so on. On the other side there is the larger number of those who toil, those without property or with little of it who by their labor produce the necessities of life both for themselves and for their economic superiors. History reveals to us further that this contradiction between two major classes in society resulted in struggles between them, sometimes smoldering over long periods of time, and sometimes bursting forth in violent conflicts. Thus the dominant classes in society have always had to maintain their position, and still more, the type of society which allowed them this dominance. Clearly there could be no better device, short of physical force, and supplementing it, than the theory of the static universe and all that it involves. For then their rule is fixed in the nature of things. It makes little difference if they say that God appointed them to this special place or that the world is so designed that a place is fitted for each thing and each thing should occupy its special place. In either case these existing economic relationships are the true, lasting, and final ones. Then these customs, laws, and traditions are rooted eternally in the nature of things and cannot be changed. "The laws of Nature and God" have been frequently invoked to stop those who sought social change in the interests of the masses of people. This fiction of a static world in which everything has its place has thus been an incalculable asset to the economic masters of society, for it both justified their rule of society and, when instilled patiently into the minds of the exploited, caused them to accept their sad position as something which could not be overcome, at least in this life.

Now conversely, those who were oppressed, who needed and required social change have had to believe that what existed was not necessary and fixed in the nature of things but could be changed. Karl Marx was the first to show clearly how these two philosophical views were expressions of social conflicts, and thus in the interests of the masses of working people of the world, he took over from Hegel the dialectical method, transformed it, and developed the dialectical materialist conception of the world. Furthermore, his belief that the universe is a changing one not only implies that society also changes but becomes the call to change it.

If we return for a moment to the problem with which this chapter opened—"You can't change human nature"—we will see a final illustration of permanence versus change. Ever since socialism developed in theory and practice into a world movement which threatened the whole capitalist system, theoretical leaders of the ruling class have argued that it sounds good in theory but will not work because "you can't change human nature." Without going into a discussion of what psychological changes socialism involves, we can inquire into the presuppositions of this view. Man is man, and as such he has a nature or character. This is inherent in his being man, and therefore as long as he remains man his nature is unchangeable. But what do we find in fact? Investigation reveals that man's nature has been in constant change throughout the whole course of his development from the higher animals and through his social history. We do not find, in fact, anything we can put our hands on and say, "*This* is human nature." We find instead changing patterns of behavior, the development of ever new motives for man's action. We do not know what *man* in the abstract is, but know only *men*—men living in concrete social environments which mold them in one way or another and cause them to act for one motive or another. The creation of a socialist society in the Soviet Union has given us striking and unchallengeable examples of changing human nature. New attitudes have arisen there, new motives for all spheres of human activity. The "profit motive" has disappeared, the so-called "competitive instinct" has been transformed into the socially useful form of socialist competition, and the conversion of private property in land, factories, etc., into common social property has wrought a revolution in the attitudes and actions of men, women, and children towards all their material surroundings.

The slogan, "You can't change human nature," is today simply a key device for maintaining the existing economic and political structure, even though it rests on a philosophical and scientific anachronism. It should be taken less as a supposed scientific statement than as a political rallying cry against the forces of progress.

IV. THE MEANING
OF SCIENCE

ORIGIN OF SCIENCE IN HUMAN NEEDS — THEORY AND PRAC-
TICE — SCIENCE IN THE CAPITALIST CRISIS — SOCIAL NATURE
OF SCIENTIFIC ENTERPRISE — THE KIND OF KNOWLEDGE
SCIENCE IS — SCIENTIFIC PROBLEMS, HYPOTHESES, AND
EXPERIMENTS — SCIENCE AND SUPERSTITION — PROBLEM OF
THE SOCIAL SCIENCES — CONFLICT OF SCIENCE AND RELI-
GION — ATTEMPTS AT RECONCILIATION — KANT — HAS MAT-
TER DISAPPEARED? — SCIENCE AND DIALECTICAL MATERIAL-
ISM — SCIENCE AMONG THE NAZIS — SCIENCE AND SOCIAL
PROGRESS

HAVING surveyed the two most important subjects of
controversy throughout the history of philosophy, it is
now desirable to see science in its relationship to these
philosophical conflicts and to examine its place in society. This is especially important for the understanding
of dialectical materialism, which is a philosophy of science—not, as already noted, in the sense of something
standing over and above the sciences. It is rather the
generalization of the principles science employs, the
picture of our world science gives us, the study of the
techniques or methods it uses, and the theory of its
function in the whole sphere of human social life.

There are many popular myths concerning science
and scientists that are little better than superstitious

nonsense. They begin with the idea that the scientist, with a capital S, has some special gift from the Gods by which he is enabled to fathom the holy secrets of the world. They end with H. G. Wells' belief that the scientists are the only sane members of our modern civilization (which has not been much of a success) and that they will perhaps save a small remnant of mankind whom they will lead onward to higher forms of culture. Technocracy, so popular a few years ago in America among women's clubs and certain intellectual circles, was an expression of this same glorification of the scientist and belief in him as offering us salvation from the social ills into which non-scientific men have led us. There is just a sufficient grain of truth in this idea to make it plausible. But further analysis of the questions must wait upon an inquiry into the origins, nature, and purpose of science.

Science seems to have had its humble beginnings in certain skills developed by early men in their attempts to control the forces of nature, and to order their social life. Diseases had to be cured, waterways and the seas had to be navigated. Houses had to be built, animals killed, fishes caught, and crops grown. All these tasks required certain knowledge of materials, of animal behavior, of instruments, of the human body and natural herbs. They required an understanding of the periodicity of the seasons, the prediction of storms, knowledge of the stars and of the minerals in the earth. As society grew more complex, as in Egypt, arable land had to be parceled out, and the rise and fall of the Nile forced upon men the necessity of accurate measurement of the land. The need for irrigation brought about the development of methods for raising water above its natural level. The building of palaces and the pyramids, in the interests of a ruling class guided by ancient traditions and superstitions, forced the men upon whom the task of building them was laid to construct devices, such as the block and tackle, for raising heavy stones.

We know that practice cannot develop far without theory, or in other words, that the practical manipulation of things cannot advance far or for long without an understanding of the things dealt with and the processes involved. Thus men of the leisure class, such as the priests in Egypt, were led to study and speculate concerning the principles already in use in measuring land and in building temples. These theoretical developments in turn led to new practical applications and hence to new theoretical problems to be solved. Among the Greeks, however, these two sides or phases of one and the same understanding and use of nature drifted further and further apart because of the difference in social status between those who performed these respective labors. Theory and practice came to be separated, and Aristotle and his contemporaries loftily looked down upon the artisan or craftsman and made a disastrous distinction between knowing how to do things—changing the world—and understanding it. As a result, there came to be what Francis Bacon in the seventeenth century called two dispensations or streams of knowledge. One of these was the traditional learning handed down through generations of scholars who knew nature only at second hand through the books of the church and ancient writers. The other was the direct knowledge of nature built up through centuries of the actual manipulation of things for man's daily use. Beneath this there really lay the conflict between philosophy as either a substitute or support for traditional religious faith and what we know as science. Bacon believed that "human knowledge and human power meet in one," and that if nature is to be commanded it must first be obeyed. Accordingly, he advocated scientific inquiry and experimentation and even envisaged in his *New Atlantis* the organization of science on a vast social scale to enlarge the "bounds of Human Empire."

It is not hard to see how Aristotle got the notion that understanding and manipulating are completely independent acts. He lived in a slave society where there was actually just such a division of labor, and his distinction is the expression of that division. He was merely describing what he saw in the society in which he lived. On the one side was the pure *knower,* the Greek gentleman who, freed from the daily economic struggle, regarded his own pursuit of contemplation as the end and purpose of human life. On the other side was the artisan or craftsman, the builder of ships and hewer of marble, who as a slave, or just up from slavery, was a member of the lower classes in society. In the sixteenth and seventeenth centuries the rising middle class in certain European countries found this distinction a hindrance to it in its struggle against feudalism and for the mastery of nature in ocean commerce, mining, irrigation, etc., and attacked this separation of theory and practice. Bacon was representative of this. So was the alchemist-chemist and physician Paracelsus who, denouncing the be-gloved physicians and professors with sleek countenance, extolled those who worked at fiery furnaces with soot-begrimed faces and calloused hands. It was these, he said, who were really studying nature in their efforts at separation and combination of the minerals and at other laborious activities in transforming nature in the interests of metallurgy and medicine.

But as capitalism developed and created new class distinctions, the old separation between theory and practice reappeared. Already by Newton's time, in the latter part of the seventeenth century, the new theoretical developments had become so separated from the practical problems out of which they had arisen that his great work, the *Principia Mathematica,* appeared to men to have been spun out of his own head as if by divine inspiration. The development of modern imperialism still further increased this disparity by concentrating capital in the hands of a few, far removed from the actual processes of production, and reducing to paid employees all those who actually operated the industries and conducted scientific research. One of the results for scientific progress was that the profit motive was placed in control of invention, and developments which did not appear directly profitable went unfinanced. Interestingly, at the beginning of the imperialist epoch in America, it was left to a theoretically untrained

newspaper vender and telegraph operator to develop
the incandescent lamp and the phonograph, and to two
bicycle mechanics from Dayton, Ohio, to build the first
practical flying machine.

The physical sciences were once the beloved child of
capitalism. Much that they are today they owe to the
fact that the capitalist class needed their service for
their conquest of nature and the competitive demand
for large-scale production. The elaborate endowments of
our universities, which had been founded and financed
originally largely by the churches, came in great part
from capitalists for the promotion of scientific research
and the training of a technical personnel for industry.
Recent scientific progress has remained closely cor-
related with the fortunes of capitalist industry. When
the world crisis of capitalism burst upon us in 1929, a
new note was sounded. Talk arose of a moratorium on
science and scientific invention. The heads of institutions, which once received beneficent funds from finance
capital, found themselves advertising their wares and
begging for contributions. Karl Compton, for example,
President of the Massachusetts Institute of Technology,
in a paper read to the 1936 convention of the American
Association for the Advancement of Science, on the subject of the social significance of the electron, made
much of the point that research in atomic physics is
profitable to capitalists because of the vast amount of
expensive apparatus used and the new industrial possibilities it opens up. But as John Strachey put it:
"What, for example, is a harried capitalist who cannot

sell, say 10,000 tons of steel a year, to say to the scientists who can tell him how to produce 1,000,000 tons?" The same is true with the farmer and the agricultural expert. The American department of agriculture employs experts in experimentation with soils and seeds to increase the yield, and at the same time under the A.A.A. the Federal government signed agreements with farmers to plow under every other furrow and in other ways to curtail production. In a world where millions are unemployed scientists are still bending their efforts to dispense with half of those who are still employed. Now what does capitalism propose to do? It wants to call a halt upon inventions that are not profitable to it, it buys them up in order to suppress them, and withdraws its support from research institutions which no longer serve its interests. Most of the scientists still think in terms of adjusting science to capitalism, but there are growing numbers who are beginning to think of adjusting the economic system to science.

One aspect of the separation of theory from practice, of pure science so-called, from the actual development of technology and the application of knowledge to the improvement of man's life, is the emphasis upon the outstanding individual in scientific advance. The individual contribution has been magnified at the expense of the long social process and cooperative labor that lies behind every significant advance in the sciences. But we are slowly coming to understand, as Professor Whitehead paradoxically put it, that no man discovers anything which was not known before by someone who did not discover it. Contrary to what we are taught in the schools, all significant inventions and discoveries are products of slow social growth. Take, for example, Galileo's invention of the telescope. Antiquity and Roger Bacon knew single glasses. Leonard Diggio and della Portia combined glasses. Jansen added the closed tube. Galileo added the reflector, and the best telescopes were produced by the Dutch guild workers by means of their socialized methods of labor. To see this today we need only turn to the great research laboratories, whether of universities or of corporations. Every worker in them knows that a discovery for which often one individual receives full credit is the result of a long cooperative labor process. The very nature of modern biological and physical research demands large scale industrial methods. In short, science always has been and is even now under capitalism, a social enterprise.

In the Soviet Union, where private capital no longer exists, great advances are made possible through the completely socialized nature of scientific inquiry in the service of the needs and interests of the whole people. The occupation of the North Pole for nearly a year by four men who studied the conditions there, captivated the imagination of the world, and the greatest explorers have had to admit the distinction between their small private enterprises, often financed disastrously by themselves or by a wealthy patron, and this social enterprise backed by the resources of a great nation. All Soviet science is socially organized as part of the life of the more than 170,000,000 people of the U. S. S. R. and is kept in the closest contact with the problems and needs of an expanding industry and agriculture. All children are educated with a scientific viewpoint, and much children's recreation takes the form of scientific study and experimentation. Workers and farmers are led to study the sciences especially as they are relevant to their particular needs, while the scientists have constant relationship in their research with developments and problems in every phase of Soviet activity. A young Soviet worker who was sent to an American engineering university was aghast when he found that an obvious error in the professor's calculations concerning the size of the firebox in a locomotive was due to the fact that the professor was using a formula in a book published in 1906. This couldn't happen in Soviet Russia, he said, where he, as a professor of locomotive construction was constantly involved with practical developments on the railroads and in the shops. This relation of science and technology in a socialist society in no way implies the abandonment of "pure" science but rather its fertilization and further development through its socialist organization and its active function in the life of society as a whole.

But just what is scientific knowledge and how is it obtained? Men hold innumerable beliefs, many of which are true, but which are none the less non-scientific. For ages men knew that opium produced sleep, that quinine was good for malaria, that gunpowder exploded, that plants turned toward the light, and that the fermentation of grapes produced wine. They also believed that the sun moved around the earth, that life was generated spontaneously in filth and decaying matter, and that heavier bodies fell faster than lighter ones. The first set of beliefs happened to have been true; the second false. But the difference between them from the standpoint of scientific method is negligible. Merely to know a fact is not to have scientific knowledge. Science is not simply knowing a truth but is knowing why it is true. It is not simply proving a fact experimentally but is connecting it in a systematic way with other truths in such manner as to provide for the detection of possible error.

Besides the beliefs mentioned above men have had other beliefs which we regard today as superstitions. Among these are beliefs that the movements of the stars control our individual destinies, that thirteen is an unlucky number, that two minds can communicate with each other without any physical means, that disease is merely a matter of our being affected by evil spirits, or by not having the right thoughts. Obviously, mankind needed some systematic guide or method by which true beliefs could be acquired and false ones avoided. Slowly over the course of the past twenty-five hundred years, such a method has been developed, and it is known as the scientific method.

The idea of science as a systematic, organized body of knowledge was expounded by Plato and Aristotle. These men saw that it was not enough merely to know a fact, to have true beliefs, but that if we are to be protected from error we must have reasons for these beliefs and know *why* they are true. Thus they insisted on proving our beliefs, that is, showing that they are true because they rest upon other beliefs that we know to be true. The trouble with this theory was that if the original beliefs were false, then everything which followed from them might also be false. Aristotle frequently said that our beliefs must be in accordance with experience and must be tested by experience, but he was only too often satisfied if his beliefs were in harmony with traditional Greek notions whether they had been put to the test of experience or not.

Clearly then, it is not enough to have good reasons for our beliefs. Something additional is necessary, namely, the testing of every belief by actual experience. When Galileo went to the top of the Tower of Pisa and dropped off different weights to prove that, other things being equal, bodies of different weight fell with the same velocity, he was doing something which any Greek could equally well have done had he only thought of it, or felt the need of thus proving a belief by trying it out in experience. From the seventeenth century onwards, it has been recognized and insisted upon that every belief concerning matters of fact must be proven by experience, and that nothing is to be accepted as true without such empirical proof. This was won, however, only after a struggle. Molière, the great French dramatist, enjoyed poking fun at the reactionaries in French medical circles in the seventeenth century, and he gives us an amusing portrait of a man who boasts that his son, a candidate for the medical degree, does not believe in the circulation of the blood or other such modern discoveries and will not accept anything as true that is not to be found in the writings of Aristotle and Galen. And we have the story of the Jesuit priest who when told by a contemporary of Galileo of having seen spots on the sun through his telescope, replied: "My son, I have read all the works of Aristotle three times and nowhere does he mention spots on the sun. There are no spots on the sun. What you see must be caused either by defects in your instrument or in your eyes." But in spite of the opposition of the reactionaries of the day, the empirical view has triumphed until today neither authority, tradition, nor reasoning concerning what *ought* to be the case is sufficient for those imbued with the scientific attitude. The scientist must produce his evidence, as must all the others who insist that something is the case.

The basic presuppositions of science were dealt with in the study of materialism. It remains now to describe certain features of the scientific method, and of the nature of proof. First of all, in science as in daily life, before there is thought there must be a problem, something to be thought about, something the answer to which one wants. Here of course, the social environment plays a large part, for the problems the scientist has to work with do not arise in a vacuum. Broadly, we can say that the problems for the scientist at any given time arise from the past history and present stage of development of any given science, in conjunction with the problems that industry and commerce, or technology in general, demand a solution of for their further development. Thomas Edison, for example, derived his problems from the need of improving telegraphic communication that growing American business created, from the need of more adequate lighting for bigger cities and larger buildings. After inventing an electric vote recording apparatus which he thought would expedite voting in Congress, he discovered that Congress was not interested in voting more rapidly but rather in delaying voting for political manœuvering. After that he was fond of saying that necessity is the mother of invention. The present work on television arises in part from the competition among the great radio companies and the need of capitalists to develop some new industry for the investment of idle money and the realization of profits. The Spanish-American War and the building of the Panama Canal forced attention upon the elimination of malaria and yellow fever, and scientists soon found the causes of these dread tropical diseases. And much of Pasteur's epoch-making work arose from the competition of the French and German beer industries.

Once the scientist has a problem, he seeks to throw as much light upon it as he can by further investigation and the use of previous knowledge. He seeks in this way to find some suggestion of a solution. This suggested solution, when elaborated, is what is known as an hypothesis, and it serves as the basis for the next step. The hypothesis is in the form: if such-and-such is the case, then when I perform this test or experiment I should get such-and-such results. Thus, when the

American doctors working on yellow fever formulated the hypothesis that perhaps the mosquito transmitted the disease, they were able to perform an experiment which would prove or disprove their hypothesis. In this case, they had to go to work experimenting on human beings who volunteered for this dangerous task. Similarly, astronomers, in the early part of the nineteenth century, when they had all the data on the movements of the planet Uranus, and found that its movements were not what they should be on the basis of the known laws of planetary motion, were led to the hypothesis that another planet, beyond Uranus, was influencing its motion. The elaboration of this hypothesis required working out in detail exactly where the supposed planet would have to be to exert just these influences. This was done by a French mathematician and astronomer, LeVerrier, in 1846, and the last step, empirical verification, was left to an astronomer at Berlin who, focusing his telescope on the part of the heavens indicated, saw the new planet, Neptune.

This last step of the scientific method requires further consideration. It is not only necessary to show that if this particular hypothesis is true, such-and-such results would occur. We must find the results and then show, as far as possible, that they would not occur as they did unless this hypothesis were true. Thus the doctors, working on yellow fever, had to perform such experiments as would eliminate every other possible cause of yellow fever except the mosquito. The method of accomplishing this is often referred to as the method of control. They put their subjects into beds in which persons had just died from yellow fever. They had them eat and drink from the unwashed dishes of fever victims. And they carefully kept all mosquitoes away. None of these people contracted the disease. They put other subjects in sterile surroundings, free from every other possible source of infection, but allowed them to be bitten by mosquitoes which had bitten yellow fever patients. These contracted the disease. In the same way Pasteur, a most ingenious experimenter, sought to prove his hypothesis that life was not generated spontaneously but that all living organisms came from other living things. He took flasks in which were preparations favorable to the development of life and contrived that no minute organisms could be present or gain admittance. He then took other flasks similar in every respect to the first, except that dust of the air could get in. In the first set of tubes no life appeared. In the second a variety of living forms developed. This method of control consists fundamentally in (1) eliminating all the possible causes of an event except the one involved in the hypothesis and (2) of bringing all of them together except the cause named in the hypothesis. Francis Bacon was perhaps the first to develop this as the method to be used in acquiring knowledge of nature. He opposed it to the method of reasoning from so-called first principles and the tendency to follow tradition and authority.

There is one further important consideration involved in the use of the technique of control. It can only be used, obviously, when we can separate a particular subject we are investigating from the rest of the world. For example, the doctors working on yellow fever had to leave out the Spanish-American War from their considerations, the extreme poverty of the Cubans, the position of the moon and planets, and so on to infinity. Now one might ask what right they had to ignore all these things. The answer is that their method worked, that their results proved successful and through them they were able to check the spread of yellow fever. But there is always danger in thus isolating any phenomenon from other things around it. We may leave out an important factor.

One modern school of idealists likes to argue, partly on the basis of Hegel's teaching of the inter-relatedness of all things, that we cannot know anything because everything is so bound up with everything else that in order to know anything we would have to know everything. Some have gone so far as to claim that no single event in the universe could be different from what it is without the whole universe having to be different. Dialectical materialism has always emphasized the inter-relatedness of things, but it does not do this *a priori*, that is, by pure reason, but through actual experience. It cannot tell us *a priori* what things are related to or inseparable from what. Scientific investigation alone can give this knowledge. How much and what features of the surroundings or environment of any given process we are investigating must be brought into the picture can only be determined with regard to each subject matter by empirical investigation. Boyle, for example, developed a formula for the relation of the volume of a gas to its pressure. This formula had later to be "corrected" for it was found that temperature was also a factor in this relationship. All science must proceed by isolating a phenomenon concerning which knowledge is sought, but it is always a major question as to what features of the environment are and what are not relevant to the behavior of the phenomenon in question. The proof of the pudding is in the eating and the vast knowledge science has acquired of nature is proved in the high degree of mastery we now have over natural forces. It is in the social sciences especially that isolation is always a delicate matter and can be a seriously misleading procedure. Political systems have usually been considered, for example, as bearing no relation to the economic structure of society. Religion is considered entirely independent of the social-economic life of a people. Studies in the arts, especially having to do with changes in art forms, have too frequently ignored related social changes. Entirely misleading conclusions can be drawn from intelligent quotients isolated from the social and economic status of the individuals involved. For decades our biology and sociology books have carried the story of the Kallikaks, two lines of descent from one father and two women, one normal and one feeble-minded. The contrasted character of the offspring of these two lines was supposed to prove inheritance of feeble-mindedness and criminality. Modern students point out, however, that these studies ignored completely the different environments of the two lines. Another example of improper isolation is found in much contemporary psychiatry in which disorders of the individual's mental and emotional make-up are treated as if entirely separate from the social conditions in which these disorders arise. This false isolationism is one expression in scientific thought of the atomism and individualism of capitalist society.

We might return for a moment to some contemporary superstitions and examine them in the light of scientific method. Most of these, such as the divining rod for locating water, alleged knowledge of distant events such as an accident to a loved one, thirteen as an unlucky number, the belief that thunder sours cream, miraculous cures at special divine places, prayer as a means of salvation from danger, are due largely to our failure to notice instances where what we expect or desire does not occur. Again, as Francis Bacon showed, men have a tendency to notice what agrees with their theories and desires, and to forget those things which do not agree. A black cat may cross our path, we might break a mirror or walk under a ladder innumerable times, and as long as nothing happens we forget it straightaway, but let once some accident befall us soon afterwards and we and all our acquaintances repeat the story as proving the belief. Coincidence is another feature in the prevalence of these beliefs. Of all the dreams men and women have concerning the fate of their distant loved ones, it would be strange indeed if sometimes the dream and the reality did not coincide. Of all the prayers that are uttered for things great and small it would be a miracle if the fulfillment of some prayers should not be realized. "I cannot disbelieve in a God who answers prayers," the preacher says. Likely as not, the evidence offered is just such a coincidence. What about the millions of prayers that went unanswered? At the cathedrals and sacred founts we do not find the crutches of those who were not cured. As Bacon said, those shipwrecked at sea do not leave mementos in the temple of Poseidon in which they had prayed for a safe voyage. The scientific method would require a thorough examination to see whether first the fact alleged actually occurred, and secondly whether it occurred for the reason given. A neurotic person suffering from a lameness or blindness which involved no organic disturbance might well be cured at the sacred fountain or by the faith healer because of his own faith and hope rather than because the fountain or healer had any special power. They might also be cured by the psychiatrist. Obviously, there is no control in all these matters, and the person who wishes to be scientific in his attitude towards the world must withhold belief.

But the question is raised, how do you know that there is not something in faith-healing, astrology, thought transference, etc.? The answer is simply that we must have evidence of such supposed phenomena, that we need not prove there is nothing in them but that it is up to those who believe to prove that there is. When Galileo discovered through his telescope that the surface of the moon was irregular, filled with mountains and craters, a church astronomer declared that it might seem to be so but it was really encased in a crystal sphere. He *knew* that the moon *must* be spherical because it was a heavenly body, the sphere was the most perfect of all figures, and heavenly bodies would necessarily have this most perfect of forms. Galileo did not need to disprove this assumption of a crystal sphere encasing the moon. Not only was there no evidence offered to support it, but the very nature of the assumption prevented its being either proved or disproved. The first rule for a scientific hypothesis is that it must be capable of proof or disproof. In other words, it must indicate something to be observed or some experiment to be performed which will provide evidence for its truth or falsity.

It is when we turn to the field of the social sciences that we find the greatest confusion and lack of clarity concerning method. This is due in part to the fact that social phenomena are far more complicated and involved and less subject to experimental examination. We cannot and do not wish to produce economic crises at will under controlled conditions in order to study their causes and consequences. Nor do we wish to create slum conditions especially favorable to the production of crime, or make another world war to study propaganda methods, shell shock, the terrorization of cities by bombs, and poison gas, or throw millions more into unemployment to gain knowledge of the influence of starvation on mental traits. But tragically, our world provides us with quite enough of these phenomena to study if we will. The problem is not merely one of the complexity and hence difficulty of the subject matter, the fact that no two events are the same, and that experiments are exceedingly difficult to perform. There is the additional factor of social or class interests. When a famous economist sought to ascribe our cyclical economic crises to the periodic increase and decrease of sunspots, he was probably not acting so much as a scientist as he was playing the part of a member of the dominant economic caste seeking to avoid the actual cause in the nature of capitalist economy. When Goebbels and Rosenberg in Nazi Germany dismiss anthropologists or psychologists from the universities it is not because these teachers are not scientific but precisely because they are. It happens that there is an irreconcilable contradiction between our scientific knowledge of the various races, their character, intelligence, etc., and the needs of the ruling German financial magnates. It would not be politic for a professor in many of our own Southern universities to teach the latest scientific materials concerning the relative abilities of the white and Negro peoples, or if he does teach them he must refrain from indicating their revolutionary social implications. Or, again, it is hardly to be expected that the individuals of great fortune and the banks which own and control the slums of our great cities should endow research into the relation of slum conditions to crime, or that Henry Ford, Tom Girdler, Eugene Grace, or J. P. Morgan should take a scientific attitude on the subject of the effect of speed-up on the health and longevity of automobile and steel workers. In short, while everyone generally is interested in knowledge which enables us to predict the weather, smelter iron, mine coal, and so on, not everyone is equally interested in scientific knowledge of the social problems which still baffle and subdue such a large part of the human race. In most of these social subjects, therefore, we find confusion of thought, repression of research, the dismissal from our universities of gifted scientists, and general backwardness in the development and utilization of scientific techniques.

Throughout all recorded history this has been the case. There have been traditions that supported the ruling classes, and institutions that maintained and guarded these traditions. When Anaxagoras said in ancient Athens that the sun was a mass of molten iron as big as the Peloponnesus, he was forced to flee from the city for his life. It was not considered proper for good Athenians to hold such heretical beliefs. And when Protagoras wrote an impious treatise on the Gods he too had to flee, and his work was publicly burned. Both of these men were expressing beliefs regarded as threatening to the *status quo,* and hence their punishment cannot be understood except as politically motivated.

In all times the Christian Church, whether Catholic or Protestant, has helped in the maintenance of beliefs regarded as *desirable* by the rulers of society. In the thirteenth century the philosophy of Aristotle was banned and his followers persecuted until Thomas Aquinas synthesized it with Christianity and made it safe. In the sixteenth and seventeenth centuries the new Copernican astronomy was under the ban and Galileo's exposition of the heliocentric theory remained on the Catholic *Index* of forbidden books until 1822. In the year 1600 Giordano Bruno was burned at the stake by the Catholic Church for his heretical beliefs, among which were those of the Copernican theory and the infinity of the universe. In the same age Servetus, a physician who helped to prepare the way for the discovery of the circulation of the blood, was burned to death in Geneva by John Calvin in behalf of Protestant orthodoxy. Galileo was forced to recant and to say that the earth does not go around the sun. Again in the nineteenth century Darwin's exposition of biological evolution started another long battle between religious forces and the proponents of scientific progress—a battle in which the famous Scopes trial in Tennessee a decade ago was but a much publicized skirmish. Today a new battle rages—that against Marxism or scientific socialism. This struggle is carried on with every variety of weapon—official silence, misrepresentation and distortion, or outright persecution—depending on the relative strength of the opposed social forces in any given place and time.

Underlying the opposition to any particular scientific development is the general opposition between the materialistic presuppositions of science and the doctrines of religion. Even though individual scientists might continue to believe in a hereafter, for example, that belief runs counter to all that science knows concerning

the world and man, as Corliss Lamont has so ably demonstrated in his book *The Illusion of Immortality.*
Science finds no God or any other so-called spiritual
power in the universe, but only the various manifestations of matter in motion. The Church may argue about
the dualism of soul and body, but all science finds is
that organisms of certain kinds are capable of thinking
and feeling. And science likewise knows no miracles, no
efficacy of prayer, no original sin, and no pre-ordained
purpose in the world. On the contrary, science presents
us with detailed knowledge of a physical world which
in one form or another always existed and shows us how
living organisms develop and function in such a world.

So much of the history of thought in the Western
European world has to do with the attempt at reconciliation of science and Christian doctrine. And steadily
theology has retreated. But this retreat has not been
simple and direct. In every step backward theology has
tried to take something away from science for payment
of what it itself has lost. Great systems of thought have
been painstakingly developed, often with little thanks
from the Church, to show in one way or another that
science is all right but still does not have the last word,
that there is a realm of the spiritual into which science
cannot penetrate, and which it must not dare to enter.
We have already shown, in the chapter on materialism
and idealism, that the latter was developed primarily
for this purpose. We can now analyze more thoroughly,
however, some of the ways in which theology has waged

its war against science, for this is much of the content of modern philosophy.

The most obvious of these methods is that of attempting to show that science supports religion and especially the Christian revelation. At one of our theological seminaries a course is given on the Virgin Birth or the doctrine that Jesus was born of the Virgin Mary. In this course materials from biology are introduced to show that parthenogenesis, or the fertilization of an egg without the male sperm, can be brought about in the laboratory in the case of a number of organisms. The conclusion is drawn that therefore the birth of Jesus in this way was perfectly in accordance with science. Here the theologians, however well meaning, have slipped up badly. They have failed to see that in introducing laboratory materials on parthenogenesis to explain the birth of Christ they have at best reduced a supposed divine and miraculous event to the level of a natural phenomenon. If it was a miracle, supernaturally brought about by the Holy Spirit, then it is beyond the province of science and the scientific material introduced was irrelevant. If it can be accounted for scientifically it loses all miraculous character and religious significance. In the same way Christian archaeologists proudly display the discovered ruins of an ancient Palestinian city as proof of the truth of the Scriptures. All they have proven is that the Bible, as the saga or epic of the ancient Hebrew people was in part a historical document which presented their history as a tribe.

Another common and obvious method is that represented by the question: "Can you prove that there is no God, no soul that is immortal, etc.? Well, then!" We have already seen that science does not feel called upon to disprove these beliefs. You could only disprove the existence of God or the reality of man's future life by empirical evidence. But by the very nature of these assumptions of religion no empirical evidence is possible (since most Christians, at least, do not accept the allegations of the spiritualistic mediums who make a business of pretending to communicate with the departed). Slightly more sophisticated is the question: "Can the scientist produce life? Well, then!" Scientists have not as yet been able to produce living organisms and it is quite possible that they may never be able to do so. They also cannot produce an electron, change most of the elements into others, or make a solar system. But man's inability to do these things is quite irrelevant to the question as to whether they can be explained by the operation of natural forces or are the results of supernatural direction. We have not found any instance of a God producing life either.

The theologian had to do better than this and he has done so. What he needed, under the conditions of modern society, was a system which would justify and uphold science on one hand and still deprive it of the power of challenging the so-called truths of faith on the other. This task was the work of an obscure teacher of ethics and philosophy a century and a half ago in the German city of Koenigsberg. His name was Immanuel

Kant, and more than any other man he has provided Protestant theologians ever since with a justification of Christian faith. Kant saw that none of the existing arguments for God carried weight. He was too rigorous a thinker and had studied too much science to regard them as at all conclusive. But having studied the British philosophers, Locke, Berkeley, and Hume, he saw a way out. He conceived of knowledge as something built up by each individual from materials received from without. But the forms or principles in accordance with which these materials were organized in order to become knowledge Kant regarded as inherent in the mind. We know the world therefore but only in accordance with these principles contributed by reason or mind regarded as something universal and the same for all thinking beings actual or possible. But what things are in themselves (Kant coined the expression *Thing-in-itself*) we cannot possibly know, since all we can know is the thing-for-us, that is, the thing as we know it or according to the principles of our thought. Science is valid, therefore, but only of the world as it is known by us. What is behind these appearances we can never know. But, Kant added in later works, we can have faith, and we have a right to believe in God, immortality and freedom of the will, since science can deal only with appearances and reason can neither prove nor disprove these beliefs because they lie outside of its province. The poet Heine says of this that Kant ushered God out the front door and then sneaked him in the back.

What Kant had accomplished was not immediately appreciated by the orthodox, and they were alarmed at his writings. He was progressive in his time and his arguments not only did considerable damage to traditional Christianity but also made impossible the deistic attempt to demonstrate God's existence from the order of the universe. Further, Kant made a special appeal to the liberals of his time through his tirades against dogmatism, the great enemy of which he posed as being. But before long the theologians and idealist philosophers had taken him up as a defender of the faith. Carlyle and Coleridge peddled him to England, others to France and the United States, while in Germany he soon had a large following. Although he made it impossible to prove God and philosophical idealism, he had made it impossible, they thought, to disprove God and to prove materialism. And they figured that this was quite gain enough. F. A. Lange, a German liberal, led a new revival of Kantianism during the middle of the last century and tried to show that Kant's philosophy made materialism forever after impossible. And ever since that time it has been popular to argue that science is all right in its place but it should not claim to know what things *really* are, also that materialism isn't a bad philosophy except that it pretends to know matter as that which is behind appearances and is therefore untenable and dogmatic. Thus Kant in the eyes of many theologians and philosophers saved the Christian faith and idealism in general from the inroads of science and the materialist philosophy. All that he really did, of course, was to create, by a fictitious analysis of the knowledge process, a false and impossible distinction between the world as we can ever possibly know it and the world as it *really* is. And in spite of the great following he has had among conservatives and reactionaries, the scientist knows no such distinction. He believes, in so far as he practices science and keeps his religion out of the laboratory, that he is investigating the nature of things and that what he discovers is the *real* nature of the universe.

There remain other forms of anti-scientific arguments developed during the past century. One group says that we can't know by science because the world is one whole, and science breaks it up and thus can never give us the complete picture. Another says that everything is so unique, so different in its inner nature from everything else that no generalizations can be arrived at. In recent years, one of the most popular arguments has been that matter has disappeared as a result of the advance of physical science and that the concept of matter is out of date. We no longer find any such thing as the early materialists believed in—hard, impenetrable particles. In their place science offers us the picture of the atom as a whirling system of forces, as composed of groups of infinitesimal electric charges moving at high velocities, with relatively vast spaces between them. This argument was answered by V. I. Lenin who, in his book *Materialism and Empirio-Criticism,* showed that this conclusion had arisen out of the ignorance by scientists of any materialism other than the old mechanistic variety. He said that "dialectical materialism insists on the approximate, relative character of every scientific proposition concerning the structure of matter and its properties; on the absence of absolute boundaries in nature; on the transformation of moving matter from one state to another...." And he added, further, that the apparent "strange discovery that mechanical laws of motion are limited to only one region of natural phenomena, while the others conform to subtler laws of electro-magnetics and so forth" is only another corroboration of the truth of dialectical materialism. It is strange indeed that in our time when scientists have come to know infinitely more about the nature of matter than was known previously, they should try to use this knowledge to argue that there is no such thing. They are like the man who, when he first saw a giraffe, denied that there was any such animal. Instead of changing their idea of matter in accordance with new scientific developments they deny its existence because it doesn't conform to their preconceived notions.

Lenin's dialectical materialist analysis of the concept of matter in contemporary physical science indicates one feature of dialectical materialism as a philosophy of science. We are now in position to expand on this theme and discuss other features of Marxist philosophy in relation to science. First of all, unlike most other philosophies, there is nothing in dialectical materialism which can be at odds with any genuine scientific knowledge. It holds that science alone provides us with knowledge of the world and man, and it recognizes no other source of knowledge than that provided by the sciences. Thus dialectical materialism is philosophy, but it is not an abstract metaphysics but the theory of human practice and the methodology of the sciences, or as Engels expressed it: "a *Weltanshauung* (world-view) which is expressed and proved . . . in all actual science."

As may be inferred from the basic Marxist principles, Marxism does not view the sciences as completed bodies of knowledge, in which everything is deducible from first principles, but as themselves historical processes as much a part of nature as the subject-matters they investigate. It is possible to explore any given science as it exists at any particular time in terms of its logical order and to see it as a deductive system. Or we can see any given science as in process of constant growth, as a temporal and dialectical process, the two poles of which are the most general principles and the most detailed concrete data. But these are dialectical poles, that is, each has meaning only in respect to the other. We do not begin at either extreme but are constantly shuttling back and forth. Our principles are generalizations of past experience and guides to future observations, experiments, and applications. And these in turn indicate further qualification or development of our theories, which again in turn refer to new experiments and new applications. This view of science helps us to avoid many pit-falls into which scientists and philosophers have frequently fallen. The moment a science is viewed statically as a deductive system the question of its truth becomes a difficult one. Many philosophers have tended to say that it is true in so far as it is a perfect logical system. But this ignores the question of its relation to, or agreement with, objective reality. And since it is patently difficult to say that any given body of knowledge is the complete and final truth about the world, these thinkers have only too easily given up all questions of the objective reference of our knowledge and accepted a position such as that of Kant. The Marxist conception avoids, or rather overcomes, these difficulties by seeing science never as a static body of knowledge but as a living human enterprise which, in its healthy state, is constantly developing, constantly increasing the scope and exactness of our knowledge of the world, thus giving us an ever closer approximation to the real nature of things.

Many scientists today, especially among the younger men, are coming to see that they need a more adequate theory of science and are turning to dialectical materialism for help. Here they find, for the first time, a philosophy which is not a metaphysics that claims to legislate *a priori* concerning the world, but a methodology which clarifies and explains the work they are doing. They find that dialectics, in its materialistic Marxist form, gives them theoretical aid in solving many of their difficult problems. Its conception of everything as in process, of the interaction of things, of the nature of change, of the autonomy of the various sciences because of the relative uniqueness of each specific kind of subject-matter, of the unity of theory and practice—to mention only a few and to avoid difficult technicalities—prove fertile ideas for scientific work. Finally, such men come to see science as a social enterprise having a social function to perform. This makes them understand the meaning of anti-scientific philosophies and movements.

It is more important to understand these anti-scientific movements in their social setting than merely to "refute" them by scientific analysis. This brings us back to the subject of this chapter: science in its social relationships. Increasingly in the modern world, maintaining the Christian religion has been really subsidiary to maintaining modern capitalist society. Many of its great political leaders have been well aware of the role of religion in upholding traditions useful to the development and continuance of capitalist economy and the whole political and social structure built around it. Alexander Hamilton wrote a terrific diatribe on the French Revolution in which he connected the attack on private property with the deist attack on the sabbath and on Christian revelation in general. Many have seen, furthermore, the importance of religion as a means of keeping the masses of people content and unrebellious. Then too, after Marx, by rigorous scientific methods, demonstrated the inherent contradictions in capitalism and its inevitable downfall, or rather overthrow by the working class, the methods of science by which such things could be proven fell more and more under suspicion. It proved far easier to adjust traditional beliefs with Darwinian evolution than it did to reconcile them with Marx's findings concerning the dynamics of capitalist development and its inability to overcome the contradictions contained within it.

In our day, with the development of imperialism, the advent of fascism, and the threatened imminence of a new world war, the ruling class has shown itself willing even to forego the advantages of that science which originally made capitalism possible through the increase of man's mastery over natural forces. Thus we find, as is to be expected, that in the fascist countries, where the contradictions of capitalism have reached their most extreme form, resulting in the most savage oppression, materialism is banned and true science is in ill repute, except in so far as it can contribute to the growth of military power and the suppression of the people. On German Empire Day in 1936 a professor at the University of Göttingen delivered the following Nazi views on science: "We renounce international science. We renounce the international republic of learning. We renounce research for its own sake. . . . We teach and learn the sciences not to discover abstract laws, but to sharpen the implements of the German people in competition with other peoples." This statement raises many serious questions concerning the nature of science, its relation to human social life, and its position in the social and international conflicts of our day. The idea of the sole purpose of science being to increase competition between modern imperialist states requires a re-examination of the ends science can and should serve.

"International science," the "international republic of learning" are renounced because the objective meth-

ods of science, international or common to all men
everywhere because of their objectivity, are opposed to
the interests of the dominant economic clique that rules
Germany and seeks thus ruthlessly to rule in all capitalist countries. The Thyssens and the Krupps need anti-
semitism to make the German people think that Jews
and not capitalists are their enemies and are the cause
of the miserable conditions they endure. But the scientific study of the races of mankind, anthropology, has
long since demonstrated the falsity of the ideas on which
anti-semitism rests. Anthropology, therefore, must go.
These economic rulers require for their profits that the
people should be content with low wages, inadequate
food, and housing. But materialism teaches that these
things are the necessary basis of the good life. And science shows that men can have these things, that goods
enough can be produced to satisfy these needs. Idealism
therefore must supplant materialism, and blind faith in
authority must be substituted for reason and science.
Materialism likewise teaches that there can and should
be progress and that life is preferable to death. So the
ruling class of Germany, through its agents Hitler,
Goebbels, and Goering, teaches that progress is an illusion and that there is no greater good men can seek than
death for the fatherland. This then is what is meant by
renunciation of the international republic of learning.
The abstract laws of science must be renounced precisely because they are not abstract but concrete. They
teach the truth that makes men free. In short, the
fascists must reject all that science teaches except what

is immediately *useful* in the production of substitutes for natural raw materials, for the production of bombing planes, shells, and poison gas.

Our own finance capitalists hail just such a program. Instead of the knowledge of man pitted against the forces of nature they would have the economic machinery of one country pitted against that of another. This is what the German professor meant by sharpening the instruments of the German people in competition with other peoples. But the masses of men know that they will fare better through international cooperation than by such competition. They know that they can and will have a better life and that knowledge and science alone can point the way to this. Today science belongs to the forces of progress, and to the forces of progress belongs the future.

V. HISTORY AND FREEDOM

DOES TIME MARCH ON? — IS ALL FOR THE BEST? — THE
CHRISTIAN THEORY OF HISTORY — RETURN TO THE PRIMI-
TIVE — GREAT MEN IN HISTORY — HEGEL ON HISTORY —
DIRECTION OF HISTORY AND THE DRIVING FORCE — THE
MARXIST CONCEPTION OF SOCIAL DEVELOPMENT: HISTORI-
CAL MATERIALISM — ETHICS, ABSTRACT AND CONCRETE —
FREEDOM — WHAT FREEDOM IS NOT — THE REAL MEANING
OF FREEDOM — FREEDOM AND HISTORICAL MATERIALISM

WHEN Professor Seligman of Columbia University
doubted whether economic crises could ever be elimi-
nated but hoped their disastrous effects could be re-
lieved, he probably did not realize that he was implying
a conception of history similar to that expressed by
Henry Ford when he exclaimed, "History is the bunk!"
Several thousand years ago the Prophet Ecclesiastes
wrote, "There is nothing new under the sun." And centuries later the Christian Church said to its followers,
"The poor you will always have with you." Today in
the same vein many people unthinkingly believe that
capitalism has always existed and always will.

These attitudes of disbelief in progress, in fundamental social change, represent one pole of the philosophy
or theory of history. This position is an expression of
the static conception of the world we have already examined. Those who have ruled society have never been

able to believe that their power could be shaken or any real change brought about. Seeking to keep things as they are, they created a conception of history to support their desires. At the opposite pole stand all those who have believed that in one way or another time marches on, that the future will not resemble the past, and that for better or worse human society changes. These range from those who cry that the world is going to the dogs, to those who believe in the promised Millennium when Satan will be chained up and peace and goodness will reign on earth. Let us examine these views of social change to see the goal towards which various thinkers have thought the world was heading, the force that drives society onwards, and the conception of human good involved. When we turn to theories of history we find that they are all conditioned or determined by the conceptions men have of what human life ought to be, that is, of what constitutes a good life.

Here again we meet as the dominant idea in the Western world for the past two thousand years, the Christian conception which finds the goal of life not in this world but in another. Just as the individual life on earth is but a preparation, a trial, for the life to come, so is the whole history of mankind a movement towards some final divine intervention whereby history will be brought to a close and the curtain will descend on the drama of the universe. As untenable as this conception is in its belief in another world that gives meaning to this one, it has helped significantly to create and to keep before men the idea of there being some meaning to life and a direction to the course of man's history.

The central problems of a theory of history have been: is there a direction to human social development, that is, to history, what is this direction, and what is the propelling force that moves society in this direction? Assuming for the time being that there is a direction, we find the most divergent views concerning the propelling force. The predominant tendency among intellectuals since Plato and Aristotle has been to assume that somehow or other there is a force in the world which willy-nilly pulls men forward. This is described technically as a teleological conception, meaning that the end or goal of history operates to move things in this pre-determined direction. Put in another way this means that history operates to produce this end in a manner similar to that in which men plan a goal, such as the building of a house or the production of a constitution. This conception can best be described as anthropomorphic, that is, as a conception of the world or nature by analogy to man's way of acting. Thus it is really an idealistic or spiritualistic theory, since it conceives of this force as similar to human will or purpose. According to this view everything that happens must have some purpose, or else it would not have happened, or, as Aristotle put it, nature does nothing in vain. He even went so far as to liken the method whereby nature brings something to pass to the way in which a man builds a house, that is, by a plan conceived beforehand of what the house is to be like and which thus determines the various steps involved.

The Stoics developed a similar view. They conceived of the world as being guided by reason so that whatever happens must be rational, hence for the best, and men have only to do their duty. This was an excellent philosophy to make men forget social inequalities and class distinctions and thus it was appropriate that its two leading representatives in the Roman world should be Epictetus the slave and Marcus Aurelius the Emperor. Stripped of all superfluities, Stoicism as a philosophy of history comes down to the belief that whatever happens must be for some good reason, and therefore we should not complain. It is easy to see how Christianity took over this same attitude and came to fulfill the same purpose. In Mohammedanism we find the will of Allah substituted for "reason" and the Christian God as the directing force of history. But even more than Stoicism and Christianity the religion of Islam stresses the utter fatalism of events and the impossibility of mere man accomplishing anything not "on the books" from all eternity. To this day, for example, the Mohammedan peasant resists the modern practice of spraying fruit trees for protection against insects, on the ground that if Allah wants the fruit to be good it will be good, and if not it won't.

In modern times Calvinism developed an equally fatalistic view. The New England Puritans, imbued with this doctrine, saw God's hand in every event. They conceived of themselves in America as constituting a new outpost in the age-old struggle against the forces of Satan, as planting God's banner in this, the Evil One's own territory. This conflict, and every encounter in it from an Indian battle to a smallpox epidemic, was planned by God from all eternity, and the Puritans regarded themselves as privileged in having been elected to participate in this great struggle which they were destined to win. Tragically, when things grew darker, and the prospects of victory dimmed towards the close of the seventeenth century, their leaders, the Mathers, taught that soon God would intervene overtly, destroy Satan, and bring halcyon days upon them. But besides its fatalistic character, Puritanism was distinguished by its unwitting revival of an ancient religious view that deserves attention.

This was the religion of Manicheism that arose in Persia and for a time was the greatest competitor of early Christianity. For the Manicheans the world was the scene of an age-old struggle between the forces of good and evil, personified in light and darkness. Man's life was the center of this cosmic duel and each man must take his stand on one side or the other. The famous Christian Saint, Augustine, was originally a Manichean and ·he carried over some of its attitudes into Christianity. He saw the whole scene of man's life as a battle between the forces of righteousness, which he called the City of God, and the forces of evil, labelled the City of Satan. The battle between these two camps, the children of God and the children of the Devil, was the meaning of history and the clue to the events taking place in the world around us. In spite of the supernaturalism of this view, the reference of the struggle to spiritual powers beyond the world of nature, it made one important contribution which does not require much imagination to envision: the good life comes only through struggle and the history of man's life on the earth is the history of the attempts at improving this life against the forces of evil. Augustine's ideas provided at least a dynamic conception of historical development in which conflict played an essential role. Stripped of its supernatural elements it allows for social progress through the play of opposing forces.

In the early modern period, among the classic philosophers, such as Hobbes, Descartes, and Spinoza, philosophy of history played a very minor part. Their static conceptions of the universe left little place for a theory of human progress. But as we have seen earlier, out of the French Revolution a new conception of social evolution was born and the idea of progress began to hold sway over men's minds. There was a reverse side to this picture too. In Rousseau's theory man was originally created good and became evil through corrupt social institutions. Back to nature, to the primitive, became the rallying cry of the romanticists. Although this has become a reactionary movement in our day, it originally was a revolutionary one, calling for the overthrow of the institutions and conditions that corrupt mankind. The French Revolution awakened men's minds to the idea of progress, of unlimited possibilities for the advancement of human life, individually and socially. And the way in which improvement was to be brought about was through education. Education of the masses through the teaching of the great new developments in science would destroy the superstition which the Church had fostered and would awaken men to the future that lies ahead. The cry was taken up in America in the period following the American Revolution and especially after the events of 1789 in France. Elihu Palmer, a blind ex-minister, was its champion and he organized clubs throughout the eastern cities for the propagation of these doctrines.

As yet there was still no adequate theory of just what progress consists in and how it comes about. Thomas Carlyle, the English essayist and historian of the French Revolution, spread widely the view that progress is brought about by great men. These great men, or geniuses, somehow arise and leave their imprint on history through their intellectual superiority. This view, of course, doesn't leave us much to do about it, except to hope and pray for the great men to come and lead us. This notion also had a certain idealistic feature. These great men are great by virtue of the possession of more mind or spirit than the rest of mankind, and it was easy to go on from this point to the notion that the masses of people represent matter while the genius is the embodiment or incarnation of mind.

At this point we must turn again to the philosopher Hegel. He admitted that great men play an important part in history, but trying to envision things in their interrelationships, as we have already seen, he saw that there was a peculiar relationship between the actions of the so-called great man and the needs of the time or situation in which he functioned. Thus he saw the great leaders of history as men who sensed the needs of their time, saw the next step logically dictated by the force of events, or in Hegel's words *"what was ripe for development,"* and concentrated all their energies on taking this step. He is reported to have said, in describing the victorious entrance of Napoleon into Jena, that he saw the World-Spirit on horseback. By this he may have meant that the Napoleonic wars were the logical step in historical development and that thus Napoleon was the instrument of that force which operates in producing social change. Hegel worked out his views in systematic form for classroom lectures which were later published under the title, *Philosophy of History.* His system is a zealous attempt to formulate the direction and driving force of human social development. It contains many brilliant observations which were shortly to be of use to Marx and Engels, the theoreticians of the working class.

First among his ideas is that of history having a definite pattern and direction. It is moving towards freedom. The succession of civilizations is not mere repetition in new form, but represents the attainment of greater or wider freedom. This progress continued until his own day, which Hegel thought was characterized by the idea of human social equality, the freedom of all men. Unfortunately, Hegel the idealist did not—he could not because of his idealistic starting point—analyze freedom concretely, did not try to see what it meant to this and that man or group of men in terms of the concrete problems of daily life. To him it was always freedom in the abstract. But it had this one important merit, it was not a mere freedom *from* restraint, but a freedom *for* something, freedom to attain our ends. The second important idea of Hegel on history is that its driving force is the needs, passions, and interests of men. The implication is that social change comes about as a result of a growing incompatibility between exist- ing institutions and new conditions which are not in harmony with them. In this way an outworn set of in- stitutions is overthrown and a new and more adequate one set up in its place. This new social order in turn breeds its own new contradictions and heads towards its own downfall and replacement by a more adequate order. But here again Hegel failed to analyze the process concretely, in terms of the actual social, and especially economic forces involved. And it was in keeping with this failure that Hegel brought the process of history to a close with the Prussian state of his day, whose faithful servant he became. One other important weakness of Hegel's theory of history is worth noting, especially for the light it throws on the achievement of Marx. On the one hand Hegel found history moving towards freedom. On the other he found that men's actions proceed from their needs and passions. The important question at once arises: how are these two related, the goal and the driving force? Here the weakness of Hegel's idealism reveals itself, for the only answer he can give is that it is the nature of Spirit to move towards freedom—freedom is its very essence and in it Spirit finds its realization. This is nothing more nor less than to say that history just moves as it does and is a miracle beyond our comprehension.

Marx and Engels as young men in Berlin studied Hegel's philosophy, pondered over it, and attempted to adjust it to the problems of their day. And for these men the central problems were those of the poverty and misery of the masses of people and their exploitation by the capitalist class. Slowly they formulated, during the 1840's, their own conception of history, its direction and driving force. They found its direction to consist fundamentally in the ever increasing mastery of the forces of production; that is, in man's growing ability to produce the goods necessary, not only for his mere subsistence, but for ever advancing standards of life. They found that capitalism was superior to all previous societies in this. It had developed the forces of production through large-scale industry and the mastery of the machine. But they believed that capitalism was beginning to outlive its usefulness in this respect. The competition for profits that the private ownership of the means of production involved, forced on one hand the constant development of machinery and improvement of the productive processes. But on the other hand, it entailed economic crises and the growing inability of capitalism to utilize to the full the very instruments of production it had developed. And they came to the conclusion that only socialism, that is, the social ownership of the means of production, could carry further the development of the productive forces and thus the material and cultural improvement of the human race as a whole. Generalizing from the contemporary scene, they found the direction of history in man's growing mastery of the forces of production, that is, his ability to produce the means for his subsistence, providing ever greater abundance with less labor. It may be noted that this is not dissimilar from Hegel's conception of freedom as the direction of history. The vast difference is that this conception is concrete, the freedom to actually attain a better life by mastery of the forces of nature and the control of social organization.

As to the driving force that moves history in this direction, Marx and Engels found it in the contradictions that have arisen in various successive forms of society, between the existing economic relations and the further development of the productive forces. But this contradiction by itself is not what drives history onwards. It operates through men in an economic class who are brought into struggle against the class that controls the existing economic process. In this way, said Marx and Engels, the rising middle class struggled for control of society against the landowning class that held the reins of power under feudalism, and finally conquered and established its own order of society. But now capitalism was not only unable to utilize fully the productive machinery that it was developing but was giving rise to a vast working class which would be led by its situation into struggle against the capitalist class and would eventually overthrow it. In short social or, more specifically, class forces, are what drive history onwards, and historical change is brought about through this struggle of economic classes seeking to satisfy their needs. Thus Marx and Engels solved Hegel's dilemma. Instead of the mysterious relationship Hegel left unexplained between history's direction and its driving force, there is now an organic unity. The very needs and interests of men of a given economic class lead them to act in such a way as to satisfy these needs and thus to advance our productive forces. This is as true of the "robber barons" of America of the second half of the last century as of the leaders of the American Revolution or of the working class struggling against capitalist exploitation. History has a direction but it has it in virtue of the nature of man's social life on the earth, and not for the metaphysical reasons Hegel gave. And not only did Marx and Engels give a theory of how history in fact had moved forward, but they were able to predict future developments and to help the working class to accomplish its historical mission. Interestingly, Hegel had taught that nothing can be learned from history. This was a logical idea in his system because of his complete separation of the direction from the driving force, and it was true that men could not profit by history as Hegel taught it. Marx and Engels, however, through their historical materialist theory were in a position to show men how they could learn from history and use historical knowledge in the struggle for social progress.

Marx and Engels, unlike virtually all others who saw a direction in social development, did not finish with the vision of society reaching some "perfect" stage and stopping there. They did not attempt to predict elaborately concerning the nature of the socialist society which would follow capitalism. Nor did they ever conceive it as arriving at some perfect stage and there coming to rest. They maintained, on the contrary, that in our present stage of history we are unable to predict precisely concerning future stages, since they are too different from our own. In this they differ sharply from all who created visions of a perfect future society, a utopia, and who attempted to describe it as a fixed and static type of social organization. All that Marx and Engels felt that scientific method allowed them to say, was that man would continue to master the forces of nature, attain ever higher stages of physical and cultural well-being, and would himself, together with his social relationships, be changed in the process.

This is only one phase of the Marxian interpretation of history. It implies, however, the other and more widely known side of their thought, the whole of which is known as the materialist interpretation of history or more commonly referred to as historical materialism. This was developed as part of the Marxian materialist philosophy in opposition to idealistic or spiritualistic theories of social change. For Hegel it was the World-Spirit, the reason inherent in the world, which had its own way of developing or unfolding itself, which led history onwards. Now whether it is such a World-Spirit, a God, or great men as the pure embodiment of reason, such a position is in opposition to materialism, which holds that matter is fundamental and that thinking and feeling are activities of highly organized material beings. Marx was led, therefore, in keeping with his materialist philosophy, to look for *material* conditions as the cause of the ideas men have, and for material social conditions as the cause of their social ideas. Or, as he put it, just as being determines consciousness, *social being determines social consciousness.*

This theory has been so much misunderstood that a little elaboration and illustration are in order. We must first understand more clearly what it was that Marx was opposing. He developed his interpretation of history in opposition to all idealistic theories, and the central feature of these is that the idea or thought, mind or reason, is regarded as the cause of social change. This is the view held today by most religious people, and all idealistic and pragmatic philosophers. William James, who is often heralded as the founder of pragmatism, made "will" or "faith" the basis of all social action and the cause of social change, and the fascists copied him in this. All that is necessary is to will a certain thing or have faith in it and we can make it come to pass. Men such as George Sorel have, on this basis, substituted for Marxism a philosophy which denies the validity of any science of society and asserts rather that "myths" or convenient fictions must guide our conduct. John Dewey, likewise, in insisting that the proposition or hypothesis that works is the true one tends to deny an objective and independent reality and to make the real a creation of thought itself. Somewhat similarly, we are told from pulpits and in the philosophical text-books that spirit comes before matter and that we must first be reformed inwardly before we can improve outward conditions. The reason the world is in such a sad state as it is now, is because men have sought the flesh-pots and forsaken things of the spirit. Christian Science, so-called, has carried this to such lengths as to maintain that evil, sickness, even death itself, are due to spiritual shortcomings and that if we could think the right thoughts they could be done away with.

The Oxford Movement in religion is the leading advocate today of this point of view as applied to social problems. All evils can be overcome if only we surrender ourselves to God and let Him lead us. This amounts to a denial that there are any contradictions in society, such as those between the interests of capital and labor, fascism and democracy, etc., and it assumes that the right spiritual attitudes can of themselves solve all problems. This view was well indicated when the Reverend Samuel Shoemaker exclaimed in a sermon during the great automobile strike of 1937: "Why don't John Lewis and Alfred Sloan listen to God? He knows how to settle the strike. . . . God has a plan for the motor industry in America. He will reveal it to obedient men."

What Marx wanted to show is that men's ideas do not just come from nowhere and then cause material conditions but that these ideas are themselves the products of particular social (material) conditions, and then in turn react upon them. Joseph Stalin expressed this lucidly when he said, in an interview with Emil Ludwig: "Marxism does not deny that prominent personalities play an important role, nor the fact that history is made by people. ... But of course, people do not make history according to their own fancy or the promptings of their imagination. Every new generation encounters definite conditions already existing, ready-made, when that generation was born. And if great people are worth anything at all, it is only to the extent that they correctly understand these conditions and know how to alter them. If they fail to understand these conditions and try to change them according to their own fancies, they will put themselves in a quixotic position. So you will see that precisely according to Marx, people must *not* be contrasted to conditions. It is people who make history, but they make it only to the extent that they correctly understand the conditions they found ready-made, and to the extent that they know how to change those conditions."

The Marxist interpretation of history was scarcely advanced, when vulgarizations of it appeared in the form of what is known as *economic determinism*. This is the doctrine that men act solely from economic motives, that is, for personal monetary gain, and it is an historical product of mechanistic materialism rather than of the richer dialectical thought of Marxism. Men of this school interpret every historical event and every action in the world around us as derived directly from each individual or group's financial interests. There is a large element of truth in this assumption and it has considerable plausibility. But it is based on two pre-suppositions that are untenable. One is that the sole motive power in human life is the acquisition of wealth. This is as one-sided as the view that men act solely to secure power over others, or that they act solely for unselfish ideals. It is itself a product of the capitalist system with its emphasis on economic gain and its system of distribution of the good things of life in terms of the money that individuals are able to acquire. The fact is that men act out of very complicated motives, among which the purely economic may or may not play a dominant role. The second presupposition of economic determinism is that men are rational in all their actions, that is, that each man shrewdly and carefully calculates what he wants and the best means of obtaining it.

The simplest examination of the actions of the men around us will convince anyone that economic determinism is not an adequate explanation of human history. We find men acting most irrationally, in terms of what they themselves in the long run desire, and shifting from this goal to that as passing circumstances dictate. This supposition, too, is a product of capitalist society in its early English heyday when men thought that if each man would only act carefully and deliberately to get what was really best for him, all would be well with the world. But if modern psychology has shown us anything, it has taught us that men are only in part, and often in small part, rational animals, and are conditioned in their behavior by innumerable non-rational factors. Still economic determinism played for a time a progressive role in the interpretation of history. In the hands of men like Charles A. Beard it led to a re-examination of our American history in terms of the economic motivations of the men who founded our Republic and thus accomplished much in breaking down the traditional belief in the pure idealistic goodness of the American Fathers and their hereditary and class descendants. But today it tends to be used more and more as an instrument of cynical negativism, attacking as narrowly personal and selfish the motives of working-class and other progressive social leaders. Such an economic determinist interpretation is not only false but perniciously misleading, in that it ignores the complex motivations of men and fails to recognize that ideals may themselves become motivating forces, as is the case with many scientists, intellectuals, artists, and social leaders. It especially fails to recognize that a man may sacrifice his personal interests for the welfare of his class.

Furthermore, it has become increasingly evident with the continued application of Marxism to historical problems that the economic determinists, in interpreting history in terms of the economic motives of individual men, fail to grasp and make clear the movements of class forces in making history. This limitation again reveals itself in the complete inability of men like Beard to understand the shifting of forces in the world today—a shifting that involves new orientations and a new line-up of progressive and peace-desiring forces against those making for fascism and war. Economic determinism, by impugning the motives of those who would thus collaborate, instead of analyzing the problem to be solved and examining the forces which are available, makes all progressive socially desirable alliances impossible.

Historical materialism, on the other hand, as developed by Marx and Engels, means first, that men's ideas are a product of their social environment, and secondly, that the most basic factor in any environment is the mode of production or the economic organization of men for the purpose of production. It is the second of these that requires further analysis. Marx has been accused of *reducing* all human actions and ideas to the economic factors of society, or, in short, to economics. This is a gross misunderstanding. In the first place, what Marx sought was not *reduction* of something more complicated to something simpler, as analyzed in the preceding chapter, but an understanding of what causes what. In the second place, these critics assume a dualism between men's ideas and their economics which Marxism does not allow. For Marx economics was not the study of things, of non-human events, but precisely a study of the economic relations of men—the ways in which men are related one to another in the process of producing the goods that satisfy their needs. Thus he was not in any sense *reducing* human relationships to something not human, but was showing that some human relationships, namely, those involved in production (economic) were of fundamental importance in determining the others, such as legal systems, political institutions, moral ideals, philosophies, etc. We cannot here go into the involved logical and historical evidence for this view. It is enough now to show that it is quite reasonable to believe that since men, in order to think, to have ethics or law, to build governments, or create philosophies, must eat and drink, must have shelter and the means for reproducing their kind, that the ways in which they are organized for doing these fundamental things will reflect themselves in the thoughts they think, the moral principles they devise, the forms of government they build, or the conceptions of the universe they formulate. And that is precisely what Marx and Engels had in mind.

We are now in a position to examine as a whole the materialist interpretation of history. History has a direction and can be seen as tending, in the long run, towards ever greater mastery and control of the means of production. This greater mastery is brought about step by step through the contradictions that arise between the forces of production and the economic relations at any given period. These contradictions are manifested in the struggle of antagonistic economic classes. This struggle takes place between the class which has control of the existing economy and the class which, through its struggle against oppressive conditions, is forced to seek control in order that the productive forces can be expanded and carried forward in its own class interest. But in the case of the proletariat, its class interest requires it to socialize the whole machinery of production and thus to liberate all society by putting an end to the exploitation of man by man. This involves, of course, as Marx pointed out, that the proletariat in liberating itself puts an end to itself as a class and establishes the class-less society. Thus the working class in struggling for the overthrow of capitalism is the emancipator of all society, unlike the bourgeoisie which could attain power only at the expense of the masses of people who would be its wage slaves.

The Marxist theory of history has the advantage over all other theories in that it conforms to the actual facts of history and the world around us; it shows the actual means or forces whereby change and progress are brought about; and it enables us at a given stage of historical development both to predict the next stage, and to throw our weight towards bringing it about, that is, to join with those class forces that are struggling towards control of the productive process for its greater mastery. Today this means the united efforts of the working class, in collaboration with all other progressive forces, for the democratic operation of our vast and complex industrial machinery. And since democracy in industry means eventually the democratic ownership of the forces of production, and their operation for the common social good rather than for profit, this means joining in the struggle for socialism, or the common social ownership and operation of the productive machinery and of all natural resources. Of course, as individuals we are "free" not to join in this struggle, and to keep aloof from the movement towards industrial democracy and socialism. But the materialist interpretation of history also shows that in any given period, and especially in a period such as ours today when the social forces are lining up ever more definitely for a decisive conflict, there are in the end only two opposed positions that can be taken. One leads towards the next historical stage, the other towards reaction. And history and Marxist political economy teach us that reaction cannot triumph forever. Fascism, for example, may hold the stage in parts of the world today, but it is destined to fall because it cannot solve the contradictions of the capitalist economy and thus meet the needs of the vast body of the working class, the farmers, and the professionals and intellectuals. And these groups, driven on by the ideas that their social position and common needs force upon them, will grow stronger in their determination to overthrow the system that oppresses them until they find the power to end it in fact.

To conclude, Marx and Engels created a philosophy of history, historical materialism, which makes possible, for the first time, a science of social change. It performed four great tasks which no previous theory of history had achieved. It accounts, first, for the origin and change of human ideas and ideologies by showing concretely how they are derived from the material and social environment of men. It shows, second, that there is a direction in social change, reveals the nature of this direction, and indicates how it arises out of the actual life of men in society. Third, it shows concretely, and through detailed evidence, that the propelling force in

social change is found in the same activity of men which
creates the direction of social development or, in other
words, that the forces which move society onwards determine, at the same time, the direction of its movement. Applied to our historical epoch this means that
the proletariat, because of its exploited position in society, is the force driving towards the next step of social
development, and that this step must be the liberation
of the proletariat from exploitation—in other words, a
socialist society. Fourth, it provides through the fore-
going that means by which men can understand social
processes and thus consciously, for the first time, advance society through their own planned creative activity. It is no exaggeration to say that no previous
conception of historical processes provided this unity of
theory and practice, this synthesis of the objective process with subjective human planning. It shows at one
and the same time the inevitable direction of social
movement and how men can work intelligently and
effectively to bring the next stage about in the easiest
and best possible way. This is the application of dialectical materialism to the problems of society and history.

These considerations of the origin of man's ideologies
and of the movement of society involve us in the question of what is the good life, how it can be attained,
and what is the basis of judgments of right and wrong.
This subject is traditionally referred to as ethics. There
is really, of course, no other ethics than social ethics.
An individual in isolation, a Robinson Crusoe on a

desert island, can have no ethics. He can do neither right nor wrong. He can maintain his life or lose it, but it would be superfluous to call the one moral and the other immoral.

There are still two basic and different views as to the subject matter of ethics. According to the one, it is a matter of moral principles of right and wrong that are supposed to govern certain phases of our conduct and not others. This is a view of the oldest of existing moral codes, the Ten Commandments. These are divisible into two parts, consisting of those which tell us what to do and not to do in relation to God, and those which indicate what we should do and not do in relation to other human beings. The point that concerns us here, since we have already examined the belief in God, is that ethics is made a matter of certain principles that are supposed to govern some features of our individual behavior. Certain actions of men are, in this view, in and of themselves good. They are good because they conform to a pre-established principle. Whether this principle is regarded as being of divine or natural origin is not now important. Other actions are evil. It is to be noted that in the Ten Commandments there is no reference to why a given action is good or bad. Obviously, there was a reason, for in a tribal society such as that for which the Commandments were formulated certain actions contributed to the maintenance of the tribe and others weakened the tribe and imperiled its stability. If children should not obey their parents, for example, or men should seek other men's wives, or covet their property in animals, the social stability of the tribal community would be in danger. Yet nothing of this broader point of view or basis, in terms of which actions were to be judged good or bad, was mentioned in the formulation of the moral code.

To this day many systems of ethics are built up in the same manner. One kind of action is just, another unjust; one is fair, another unfair; one is honest, another dishonest. But in such systems nothing is said concerning what makes an action just or unjust, fair or unfair. This is the basis of much of the practice of contemporary liberals. The idea of a pure and absolute good, justice, honesty, etc., blinds them to the difference between these ideals as good because of their service to concrete social ends, and these ideals as themselves constituting the end which all else must serve. Liberals are troubled, for example, by such a question as to whether the use of force can ever be right, or whether it is just for the workers to conduct a sit-down strike and thus occupy property "which does not belong to them." Besides confusing means and ends, such people are thus demanding that the working class conduct its struggle against the capitalists in accordance with rules the capitalists themselves have formulated, and which they follow more in the breach than in the observance. Today it is a definite disservice to the cause of progress to conceive of ethics as simply a matter of obeying certain principles and to regard these principles as abstract and eternal truths.

Liberals are fond of raising the question as to whether

the end justifies the means. They do not realize that the very asking of this question assumes the existence of abstract and universal ethical truths which stand over and above the actual concrete needs of men. The question is misleading, because the real problem is not whether the end desired justifies the means used, but what really are the desired ends of life. It comes down to the question of what makes any principle or rule good. If some rule is good simply in and for itself (for example, that a man should not be deprived of his property, or that all men must at all times have complete freedom to do as they think best) then men should, at all costs to their actual social needs, observe these rules. But if what is good is judged to be so in terms of the social needs it fulfills (an economy, for example, which would eliminate unemployment, want, and war) then the only criterion of good is its success in fulfilling this need. Thus the argument of the reactionaries and liberals against "the end justifying the means" is a disagreement as to what ends are to be sought and what makes anything good. Marxists reject the proposition offered to them by such people that the end justifies the means. They hold, on the contrary, that the only thing which makes any rule an end is the service it performs in bringing about a better life. They agree with Spinoza that we do not strive for or desire anything because we believe it to be good, but rather we deem a thing to be good because we wish for or desire it. To say that something is good, in short, is to say that we want it, either as an immediate satisfaction in itself or as a means to some further satisfaction. Thus nothing is good which does not satisfy a need and those things in turn necessary to satisfy basic social needs are good. Such is the dialectical relation between means and ends, never separable, each conditioning the other at any particular time. An appropriate illustration is found in the relation of the struggle for immediate demands, for the amelioration of the condition of the working class, and for socialism. This dialectical conception of the relation of means and ends is the ethics of the working class in its historical struggle. To criticize it for not being bourgeois ethics is to forget the difference in ends: the difference between maintaining capitalist society and achieving socialism. What some so-called liberals are really worried about is the price they may have to pay during the transition period. The whole controversy is a part of the larger one concerning the origin and nature of moral rules.

This brings us to the second view of ethics, that view for which ethics is the whole problem of human life. In this sense of the word nothing is foreign to ethics. Men living together in society, seeking their needs and the fulfillment of their desires, seeking first of all the satisfaction of their basic needs of food, shelter, and clothing, and through them the further so-called higher needs of recreation, friendship and love, knowledge, the arts, the fullest development of their capacities,—this constitutes the field of ethics. From this standpoint there is no special sphere of ethics; it embraces every phase of human life and activity. It is the study of the ways and means to man's collective quest for a good, a better life. This view has the advantage over the first and more traditional one in that it holds together under the one idea of the general good all phases and aspects of human activity. It is thereby a truly human ethics. It has a second advantage. It links together as one the things that we seek as good and the means necessary to attain them. Under this view nothing can be good, and yet be "good for nothing." This is so because whatever is judged as good is judged so because it gives some positive advantage; it satisfies some human need, or it puts us in a position better to satisfy such a need. Under the traditional view something is good because it is good, and wrong because it is wrong, quite apart from the good or ends men seek.

It is to be remembered that Hegel held freedom to be the goal of life and the direction of all social evolution. Although he did not analyze this idea concretely, and thereby fell into the grievous error of upholding the Prussian state against the progressive forces of his day, there is much that is sound and suggestive in his position. But freedom must be concretely defined. This can best be done by indicating a few things that freedom is not.

First of all, freedom is not "free will," that supposed gift of God, of doubtful value, whereby a man is thought capable of choosing or not choosing anything indifferently, regardless of all circumstances, environmental influences, motives—in short, regardless of everything. Advocates of free will have generally admitted that all events in the world are causally determined save alone man's will. This they conceive as exempt from causal relations. The undetermined and unconditioned will can, they presume, make a decision in and of itself without any influence biasing it one way or the other. Neglecting the theological origins of this doctrine, it is sufficient here to show its impossibility and undesirability. It conceives of the will as a special kind of thing in us which makes choices and makes them for no reason at all. But we find in fact that *men* choose and that their choices are their response to the situation before them as motivated by their character, their ideas, etc., as these have been moulded by all their previous experience. If this were not so, society could not exist. We could not train and educate human beings because training and education would have no effect on the choices of their "free" will. We could not predict a man's or a group's behavior from one moment to another since this behavior would not be the product of conditions and past experiences. Furthermore, this view of free will is commonly used as a way of placing blame upon the individual for crime and anti-social actions in general, instead of on his environment, and thus of avoiding inquiry into the social causes of crime. Real freedom, as we shall see, lies not in such supposed non-determination of the will, but in fact presupposes the determination of human actions by habits, ideas, motives, etc., which are the products of the physical and social environment. It is in order here to quote an

analysis of this subject given by Engels in his work
Anti-Dühring:

"Hegel was the first to state correctly the relation
between freedom and necessity. To him, freedom is the
appreciation of necessity. 'Necessity is *blind* only *in so
far as it is not understood.*' Freedom does not consist
in the dream of independence of natural laws, but in
the knowledge of these laws, and in the possibility this
gives of systematically making them work towards definite ends. This holds good in relation both to the laws
of external nature and to those which govern the bodily
and mental life of men themselves—two classes of laws
which we can separate from each other at most only in
thought but not in reality. Freedom of the will therefore means nothing but the capacity to make decisions
with real knowledge of the subject. Therefore the *freer*
a man's judgment is in relation to a definite question,
with so much the greater *necessity* is the content of this
judgment determined; ... freedom therefore consists in
the control over ourselves and over external nature
which is founded on knowledge of natural necessity; it
is therefore necessarily a product of historical development."

Freedom is not the right of anyone and everyone to
do exactly as he pleases, as any whim, caprice, fancy,
overwhelming desire or madness dictates. This would
be a freedom only to be guided by emotion or passion,
by prejudice or ignorance, to be driven this way or that
as smoke is driven by the wind. Many sincere and honest
men in reacting against the pressure of outworn tradi-

tions or coercive and oppressive institutions have been led to take this view. Thoreau is one of the best examples of this in American history. Seeing our society as based on exploitation, and desiring neither to exploit nor to be exploited, he went to the woods to live, and landed in jail for non-payment of taxes. It is clear that there could be no freedom in any real sense if everyone could act as fancy dictated. We would not be free to drive cars up and down our streets or across the country if one could drive on the left side, disregard traffic signals, and the like. It would not be a freedom for the motorist to get where he wanted to go. Freedom, likewise, cannot mean the freedom of anyone to work as long hours as he chooses or for what little wages. Even though various of our courts have in the past declared unconstitutional laws limiting the hours of industry and setting minimum wages on precisely the grounds that they restricted the individual's freedom to sell his labor as he choose, it has come to be recognized that the freedom to be thus exploited is a spurious kind of freedom. The cry that has gone up from reactionary circles against the Federal Child Labor Amendment is another illustration of the misuse of the concept of freedom by the economic overlords of our society. The federal government is taking away the freedom of parents and taking the control of their children out of their hands, went the argument. These people, supported so vociferously by the Catholic hierarchy, forget that the government compels vaccination of children, school attendance, quarantine of contagious diseases, etc. It has done so because a certain security from disease and level of education have been necessary for the maintenance of our society. Even capitalism, concerned as it is with the continuance and increase of profits above all else, has been forced to impose restrictions upon individual capitalists whose malpractices, it is thought, would bring ruination upon it. Every form of society has done likewise, has restricted the individual in order to promote the greatest amount of good for the dominant class, and will continue to do so until a class*less* society is attained.

There is another misconception of freedom that must be examined before we turn to what freedom truly is. This is the view, popular in the United States, of freedom as the abstract freedom under the law for men to do certain things whether they have the power or desire to do them or not. It is the freedom of every man to own a yacht or to sleep on a subway bench. It is argued, or assumed even without argument, that every child born in the United States is free to go to school as long as his abilities allow. It is true that there is no law against it, but only a very small minority of our citizens have it within their power to continue their education beyond the elementary schools. Economic necessity prevents it, and they are therefore *not free* in this regard. At every commencement exercise of our colleges and universities the graduating students are told of the paths ahead of them that they are now free to follow. They can, thanks to the blessings of our great democracy, so the story goes, become doctors, lawyers, or engineers. They can become civic and social leaders, can become anything from the President of the First National Bank to the President of the United States. But the fact is, that even though there is no statute *law* to prevent this, there are the economic laws of capitalist society which will lead these graduates into WPA jobs, into substitute teacher positions, into miserably underpaid clerical posts, or put them on home relief. Under the law, the twelve million Negroes in the United States are as free as the whites. But we know in fact that this is not the case, that innumerable restrictions and handicaps are imposed upon them. The Jew has the same rights as the Gentile under the law. But we know that "restricted" suburbs exist and that the "Aryan" can get a job more easily. Freedom, in any real sense, can extend only so far as we have the power to fulfill our desires.

As Stalin told a conference of Stakanovites in 1935, the achievement of political freedom for the proletariat and peasantry of Russia was not enough. "If there is a shortage of bread," he said, "shortage of butter and fats, a shortage of textiles, and if housing conditions are bad, freedom will not carry you very far. It is very difficult, comrades, to live on freedom alone. In order to live well and joyously, the benefits of political freedom must be supplemented by material benefits."

Freedom, finally, cannot mean the freedom of a group or class to live and prosper at the expense of the rest of society. "Freedom to exploit" is a contradiction in terms because it implies and requires the "freedom to be exploited," which is a meaningless phrase. Yet this is the freedom that Alexander Hamilton had in mind when, in the American Constitutional Convention, he declared that "inequality of property exists among us and will continue to exist so long as liberty exists." Liberty meant to Hamilton simply the freedom of one class to exploit another. This is the freedom of Henry Ford and the Liberty League. That it is at all accepted today, by any but the exploiters themselves, is due only to the fact that the economic class that dominates a society molds its ideology or mode of thought. To people brought up in a radically different type of society, such a conception of freedom is patently absurd to the point of incredibility, as a story told by Sherwood Eddy amusingly illustrates. In a Moscow Park he became engaged in conversation with a little girl who wanted to know if it is true that in America a man can own a factory and employ tens or hundreds of workers to work for him. Mr. Eddy answered yes, that he could, adding that he can employ thousands of men to work for him. Whereupon the little Soviet girl querulously replied, "Why don't they arrest him?"

To her, educated under a socialist society, it was inconceivable that men should tolerate a situation not to their best interests. Ignorant of the political structure of capitalism, she assumed that the law and the courts existed solely for the protection and promotion of general human well-being. The freedom of the capitalist to own an enterprise was superseded, in her mind, by the broader concept of social freedom.

Freedom in the fullest sense can mean only the freedom of men collectively, living together in society, to attain the highest individual and collective well-being— to attain the fullest, freest functioning of each individual in relation to every other. This alone can be the meaning of freedom as the goal of men and the direction of history. It requires both the mastery of the forces of nature for the attainment of an economy of abundance, and the completest, most conscious, and rational control of human society itself. It means, concretely, the freedom of men to be guided by reason, that is, to act rationally. And we act rationally when we know what we want, when our wants are compatible with one another and with those of other men, and when we know the means necessary to attain our ends and have these means in our power. This is not the freedom that we have been offered by the theologians under the name of free will. It is not a will that is undetermined in its decisions, but the freedom to choose what is required for our well-being and to take the means necessary to realize this choice. It means the protection of society as a whole against the rapacity of special interests, the curbing of such interests, and the abolition of the exploitation of man by man. It is the freedom of men to act democratically in the determination of the conditions of their work and whole life.

It is not the freedom, advocated by a delegate to the New York State Constitutional Convention in the summer of 1938, of universities to bar students for racial, political, or religious reasons, nor the freedom of a citizen to exercise the "right of discrimination" against others because of their race, nor is it the freedom of anyone to exercise what this delegate called his "God-given prejudices."

Freedom, in this fullest sense, means finally the freedom to organize and operate our political and economic apparatus so that it is completely under our control and domination, giving us the goods and the ends which we desire from it. The cyclical crises of capitalism bear tragic witness to capitalism's failure to give men freedom. Because of them even the average capitalist is not free for he is unable to prevent crises or control the operation of the capitalist system. All the prayers and pious hopes offered up in the earlier years of our present crisis achieved nothing towards its alleviation. It was something not in human control. We are victims of the economic machine under which we live, not its masters. But economic science and the achievements of the Soviet Union present us with the possibility of a rational economic system which we can operate to fulfill our common social ends.

Freedom, as it has been used here, is both the end we seek and the means to that end. It is the end because it embraces concretely all those good things of life that men desire. It can never be completely attained, for it is inconceivable that all present and future desires of men can ever be satisfied. History and daily experience show us that when men reach the satisfaction of those most basic desires of food, clothing, and shelter, they go on to desire this and that particular kind of these things, and also acquire new desires for recreation, the enjoyment of art and music and literature, greater knowledge of nature and of man's life and history, new achievements in science and invention. Freedom, at the same time it is the end we seek, is the means to this end, since at every stage of our individual and social life it means the ability to achieve our desires and satisfy our needs. It means everything at any stage that puts us in a better position to reach a further stage. If our present democracy, for example, is good it is not so as the fetish liberals try to make of it, the be-all and end-all of society, but as a means whereby certain progress towards freedom may be made under particular conditions. Or, to take another example, the American Federation of Labor has in the past brought freedom to millions of American workers—the freedom to have a better life and to control the conditions under which they labor. But today this task is shared with the C. I. O. which is bringing more freedom to millions of American workers heretofore unorganized. It should be obvious to everyone that the closest cooperation and ultimate unity of these two great labor groups will be a step towards still greater freedom for the American workers. Freedom throughout the world is thus identified with everything that we mean by progress as opposed to reaction. The fight of the Spanish Loyalists and of the Chinese people, the liberation struggle of the Puerto Rican people, the anti-fascist movement in Germany and Italy, the Popular Front in France, and the steps towards a Democratic Front in America are all movements towards freedom.

The struggle for freedom is thus the struggle for individual and social progress, for everything that gives men greater power over themselves and their environment. Freedom, in fact, is power, the power to accomplish what we desire and need for a better life. And it takes reason to achieve freedom. But not reason in a vacuum, the kind of disembodied speculation or contemplation that pretends to stand above the world of human needs. It takes reason that has the courage of its convictions, reason that not merely knows what is and what ought to be but which knows this with an emotion that propels to action.

This conception of ethics brings us back to the materialist interpretation of history. History moves towards freedom as the mastery by men of the natural world and his social order. History, however, is but a name for the actual life of men viewed in its motion in time. It is not an abstract something that has its own laws of development. It is the record, rather, of man's struggles. Thus, men make their history but not out of whole cloth, not as something spun out of their heads. This is not to underestimate the important role of ideas in human behavior, but is simply to assert that what men do at any time is the product of what they are, which in turn is the result of the whole of the conditions of their lives. If human society has moved forward it has generally done so only blindly. Men were forced by their conditions into certain courses of action which sometimes brought the desired end and which sometimes failed to do so. Failure, however, not having solved the problems which initiated the struggle, led to new struggles until the need was satisfied. Thus we find that history does not present us with any straight-line development. Human progress has been marked by a zig-zag course, by long retrogressions, by slow and steady developments, and by violent leaps into the future. And this progress has been blind in large part in that men were but dimly aware of the goals they sought and the means to attain them.

Today we are entering a new historical epoch in comparison with which the past will appear as but man's prehistoric period. For we are at the threshold of history in that fuller sense of man's rational and conscious control of his destiny. Ever widening masses of men are struggling consciously and systematically for a rational social order in which all forms of exploitation will be abolished and in which the good of each will be the good of all. Knowledge of philosophy in the hands of such men will be a powerful weapon for social advancement. It will enable them to throw light on difficult problems, to avoid the pitfalls of traditional idealistic and static thought, and to clarify for themselves and others the goals they seek. In the hands of those satisfied with the existing order and opposed therefore to change, philosophy can be only an instrument for maintaining the status quo by such means as have been described. But if the future belongs to the masses of common men, then to them also and their leaders must belong that mastery of thought and facts through which alone the future is attainable.

REFERENCES

Anaximenes (6th century B.C.)
Early Greek philosopher. For Greek philosophical thought see: Burnet, *Early Greek Philosophy;* Windelband, *History of Ancient Philosophy;* Robin, *Greek Thought.* Aristotle, in Book I of his *Metaphysics,* gives an interesting account of his predecessors.

Aristotle (384-322 B.C.)
Most encyclopedic of Greek philosophers and political theorists. Taught, wrote, and conducted extensive scientific research in many fields. Collected works published in English by Oxford University Press. Of special interest to the general reader are: *Physics, Metaphysics, Ethics, Politics,* and *De Anima* (Psychology).

Aurelius, Marcus (121-180 A.D.)
Roman Emperor and philosopher. His *Meditations,* together with the *Discourses* of Epictetus, give a representative account of the Stoic philosophy.

Bacon, Francis (1561-1626)
English jurist and philosopher who attempted a reconstruction of knowledge and the formulation of a new method of scientific inquiry. His most important writings are: *The Advancement of Learning, Novum Organum,* and *New Atlantis.*

Bacon, Roger (1210 or 1215-1294)
Inspired by Arabian scientific work, he attacked reliance on authority, experimented and wrote in fields of natural science, and sought to reform philosophy. His *Opus Majus* was recently published in an English translation.

Bergson, Henri (1859-   )
Contemporary French philosopher. His *Introduction to Metaphysics* is the best introduction to his thought. His latest major work, *Morals and Religion* (English

edition, 1934) represents the reactionary implications of his philosophy as applied to ethical and social problems.

Berkeley, George (1685-1753)

Irish philosopher and Churchman. His works, in four volumes, are published by Oxford University Press. Most important to the general reader are: *Three Dialogues Between Hylas and Philonous,* and *Principles of Human Knowledge.* His *Commonplace Book* (in Vol. I of *Works*) affords interesting insights into Berkeley's philosophical development and motivation.

Cooper, Thomas (1759-1840)

English philosopher and political writer who emigrated to America with Joseph Priestley in 1794. Was active in the French Revolution and in defending it in England. Became an active Jeffersonian in this country and suffered considerable persecution for his political radicalism and philosophical materialism. His most important works are: *A View of the Metaphysical and Physiological Arguments in Favour of Materialism,* and *Lectures on the Elements of Political Economy.*

Democritus (460-357 B.C.)

Greek philosopher famous for his development of the atomic view of the world. For an account of his philosophy see references above under Anaximenes, and also F. A. Lange, *History of Materialism.*

Descartes, René (1596-1650)

French mathematician, scientist, and philosopher who sought to justify the methods and conclusions of the new physical science. His major philosophical writings are contained in the volume, *Descartes, Selections,* in the Modern Student's Library philosophy series.

Engels, Frederick (1820-1895)

Co-author, with Karl Marx, of the *Communist Manifesto,* and life-long collaborator of Marx in the development of scientific socialism. His most important philosophical works in English are: *Ludwig Feuerbach,* and *Anti-Dühring.* The pamphlet, *Socialism, Utopian and Scientific,* is a portion of the *Anti-Dühring,* supplemented by an introduction that gives in brief form an account of his materialist philosophy. Engels' *Dialectics of Nature* is scheduled for 1939 publication by International Publishers.

Epictetus (1st century A.D.)
Roman slave whose *Discourses* (Everyman's Library) provides a handbook of the Stoic philosophy.

Epicurus (341-271 B.C.)
Founder of the Epicurean philosophy, which consisted primarily of a rational way of life based on Democritus' atomic philosophy. An interesting collection of source materials on Epicurus is to be found in Book X of Diogenes Laertius, *Lives of Eminent Philosophers.*

Feuerbach, Ludwig (1804-1872)
German disciple of Hegel who turned to materialism and became a critic of traditional religion. He is known today almost entirely as a link in the transition from Hegelian idealism to dialectical materialism. His most important work is the *Essence of Religion.* Engels, in his *Ludwig Feuerbach and the Outcome of Classical German Philosophy,* published in 1888, pays tribute to Feuerbach and gives a critical account of his thought.

Heraclitus (6th to 5th centuries B.C.)
Greek philosopher, famous for his reputed conception of the world as involving eternal change through the conflict of opposites. Accounts of Heraclitus can be found in the works on early Greek philosophy cited under Anaximenes.

Hegel, G. W. F. (1770-1831)
Hegel's works are of unusual difficulty for the beginner. The most important are: *Philosophy of History, Philosophy of Right, Phenomenology of Mind,* and the *Science of Logic,* all available in English translation. The prefaces to *Phenomenology,* the *Philosophy of History,* and *History of Philosophy* are perhaps the best introductions to Hegel's work. The first two of these, together with other important materials, are contained in *Hegel, Selections,* in the Modern Student's Library.

Holbach (1723-1789)

Baron d'Holbach was a German by birth who lived most of his life in France. A thorough-going materialist and staunch opponent of Christianity, his main work, the *System of Nature,* is a sort of compendium of eighteenth century French materialism. Selected writings of Diderot, Holbach's friend and co-worker, in the volume *Diderot: Interpreter of Nature* (International Publishers) contribute to the understanding of this philosophical movement.

James, William (1842-1910)

American philosopher and psychologist who sought a new justification for spiritualist beliefs. His most popular works are: *Pragmatism,* and an essay, "The Will to Believe" in a volume of the same name.

Kant, Immanuel (1724-1804)

Is best known for the three works, *Critique of Pure Reason, Critique of Practical Reason,* and *Critique of Judgment.* The Modern Student's Library volume, *Kant, Selections,* contains materials from all three. *Lectures on Ethics* is another useful work in English. For a general introduction see Höffding, *History of Modern Philosophy,* vol. II.

Lenin, V. I. (1870-1924)

His major contribution to philosophy is the volume, *Materialism and Empirio-Criticism.* Other philosophical writings are contained in Vol. XI of *Selected Works,* published by International in 1939. The *Philosophical Notebooks* are available in a German translation from the Russian.

Locke, John (1632-1704)

English philosopher and political theorist. Locke's important philosophical· work is *An Essay Concerning Human Understanding.* His *Treatise of Civil Government* and *Letter Concerning Toleration* (published in one volume, New York, 1937) reveal Locke's work as a theoretician of the bourgeois revolution.

Marx, Karl (1818-1883)

Marx's best known work is his monumental analysis of capitalist economy, *Capital* (3 volumes). His dialectical materialist philosophy is to be found throughout this work as well as through everything else he wrote. The best available sources for his philosophy, in English, are: *Poverty of Philosophy*, preface to the *Introduction to Critique of Political Economy, Critique of Hegel's Philosophy of Right*, and the *Selected Correspondence* of Marx and Engels. The *Holy Family*, not yet translated, and the *German Ideology*, issued by International Publishers in 1939, represent Marx's theoretical development and his criticisms of his philosophical contemporaries.

Newton, Sir Isaac (1642-1727)

Newton's great work is the *Mathematical Principles of Natural Philosophy*. The General Note (Scholium) of Book III gives a brief but succinct account of his theological position.

Occam, William of (c. 1300-1349)

An English Franciscan monk who taught at Oxford and then on the Continent. Condemned for heresy twice during his life and frequently afterwards. An opponent of the traditional scholastic philosophy, Occam was an important precursor of the modern scientific viewpoint.

Plato (427-347 B.C.)

As Plato wrote only in dialogue form, a representative picture of his philosophy can be derived only from the reading of a number of his *Dialogues*. The most important of these for the understanding of his thought are: *Phaedo, Phaedrus, Symposium, Protagoras, Theaetetus, Republic, Gorgias, Timaeus,* and *Laws*.

Spencer, Herbert (1820-1902)

Staunch upholder of *laissez-faire* capitalism and disciple of Darwinian evolution, Spencer sought cosmic justification of the English economic order of his day. His most important works from the standpoint of the present are: *First Principles, Social Statics,* and *Data of Ethics.*

Spinoza, Benedict (1632-1677)

Spinoza's greatest work, *Ethics,* contains his view of the world and man and his idea of the good life. This is to be found, together with selected correspondence and other writings in the Modern Student's Library volume, *Spinoza, Selections.* His valuable *Political Treatise* is also available in English.

Stalin, Joseph (1879-   )

While a student in the Tiflis Theological Seminary, Stalin began his study of Marxism. His systematic work, *Foundations of Leninism,* and his theoretical studies on the national question, as well as his other writings, reports and speeches, reveal the application of dialectical materialist thought and method to international problems, the Russian Revolution and the construction of a socialist society.

Thales (6th century B.C.)

From the city of Miletus, on the coast of Asia Minor, Thales is traditionally credited as the founder of European philosophy. The little that is known of him can be found in the works cited above on early Greek philosophy.